IN T

BLOC

IN THE BLOOD

My life in and out of football

PAT SPILLANE

with MICHAEL MOYNIHAN

GILL BOOKS

Gill Books
Hume Avenue
Park West
Dublin 12
www.gillbooks.ie

Gill Books is an imprint of M.H. Gill and Co.

9780717197521

Designed by Typo•glyphix, Burton-on-Trent DE14 3HE Printed and
bound in Great Britain by CPI Group (UK) Ltd, Croydon, CRO 4YY
This book is typeset in 12.5pt on 18pt Minion Pro.

*The paper used in this book comes from the wood pulp of sustainably
managed forests.*

A CIP catalogue record for this book is available from the British
Library.

5 4 3 2

This book is dedicated to the most important people in my life – Rosarii, Cara, Shona, and Pat Junior

CONTENTS

Introduction   1

Chapter 1 Family Matters   3
Chapter 2 Templenoe: The Home Place   23
Chapter 3 Living Next Door to the Bishop   39
Chapter 4 Stopping the All Blacks in Their Tracks   47
Chapter 5 The Klondyke of Seventies Ireland   59
Chapter 6 Learning the Ropes   79
Chapter 7 Unbeatable   99
Chapter 8 Rats and Rehabilitation   117
Chapter 9 Bonus Territory   135
Chapter 10 Football: How the Past Informs the Future   151
Chapter 11 Dwyer   163
Chapter 12 The Men in the Dressing-Room   183
Chapter 13 Practice Doesn't Make Perfect, Perfect
               Practice Does   199
Chapter 14 *The Sunday Game*: Apologising to
               the Nation   217
Chapter 15 *The Sunday Game*: Everyone's a Pundit   251
Chapter 16 Reality and Rural Ireland   285
Chapter 17 Under the Microscope   295
Chapter 18 The People Who Count   323

Acknowledgements   339

INTRODUCTION

I called it a day on *The Sunday Game* when Kerry beat Galway in July 2022 and I surprised people when I cried live on air.

I surprised myself. I'm a private person though I've been in the public eye for 50 years. I certainly didn't plan on shedding a tear in front of a million TV viewers.

It wasn't because I was leaving *The Sunday Game* after 30 years. The send-off was great, but there were also times I had to be hidden in cars and smuggled out of stadiums to get away from angry supporters.

It wasn't because I was saying goodbye to Croke Park. Half a century before that last TV appearance, myself and a classmate from west Kerry, Páidí Ó Sé, wandered into the old ground late one night when the gates were left open and pretended we were playing an All-Ireland final and the memories only got better after that. We were on teams that brought Sam Maguire down Jones' Road eight times.

It wasn't because Templenoe had four players on the Kerry selection, though that was a fair part of it. I could remember the likes of Timmy Clifford senior, who gave his life to Templenoe, saying to me, 'We'll keep it going, Spillane,' when we were struggling to field 15 players from a small rural community. The likes of him would have been bursting with pride to see so many of his clubmen winning an All-Ireland with Kerry.

It wasn't because two of my nephews, Adrian and Killian, won All-Ireland medals that day, though that's coming close to it. Adrian had 64 written on his gloves for the game, and as I said on television, my father was a Kerry selector for the 1964 All-Ireland defeat against Galway.

He dropped dead two days later of a heart attack, so he never saw me and my brothers, Mike and Tom, play for Kerry. He missed his sons bringing 19 All-Ireland senior medals into his house. He didn't see his two grandsons win their medals. That's why Kerry and Galway in an All-Ireland final will always mean 1964 to me.

All the threads were drawn together in that minute or two after the final whistle. My father. My family. Templenoe, a small country place. Kerry, a proud county. Croke Park.

Playing football. Talking football.

I said that day on television: it's in our blood. And in our tears.

CHAPTER 1

FAMILY MATTERS

The Spillanes have lived in Templenoe for generations. My grandfather Pat Spillane had the bar first, and in due course, my father, Tom, took it over.

There were two families in the one house at one stage, which must have been a strange set-up – two families that literally lived in one building. In one part you had Jerome Spillane and his family, and on the other side was Pat, my grandfather, and his children. Jerome's grandson is Brian Spillane, who played rugby for Ireland – that was the connection: they'd be cousins of ours. There was Tom, my father, but there were plenty more. There was Dode, there was Gene, there was Paddy, and there was Kathleen and Nuala and Rose.

Long before my father took over the bar, he was sent to school – sent away by my grandfather – in St Brendan's in

Killarney. On the first day in St Brendan's, he made great friends with a man called Jackie Lyne. And Jackie introduced his sister Maura to my father several years later, and eventually Maura married my father.

Of course, the Lynes were royalty when it came to Kerry football. Denny won All-Ireland medals and captained Kerry in the All-Ireland final played in the Polo Grounds in New York in 1947 (which Cavan won, unfortunately for us). Canon Michael Lyne was chaplain of Glasgow Celtic for years. He had a couple of All-Ireland medals himself and was actually prevented playing in more All-Irelands; because of the clerical rules of the time, he wasn't allowed out of Maynooth to play. Jackie Lyne not alone played for Kerry but managed the county when they won All-Irelands in 1969 and 1970. When I say royalty, I mean it.

The Lynes were cattle jobbers, cattle dealers, and that's a race of men who know the time of day. They drove a hard bargain, going around the cattle fairs of Cork and Kerry and further afield, buying and selling cattle, and they were very successful. They knew the value of a penny, never mind the value of a pound, and that was an outlook that probably rubbed off on my mother.

When she married my father around 1952, it must have been like going from the first world to the third world for her, coming out to Templenoe. She was moving from Killarney, which was well developed for the tourist market even then, to a place where there was still no electricity, literally. The ESB hadn't yet made it out the road and wouldn't get to Templenoe until around 1954, so that was a fair difference compared to the literal bright lights of Killarney that she was used to. It must have been one hell of a culture shock. She was busy, at least. My father had the bar but he was also a hackney driver, and there were petrol pumps and a shop there as well.

I didn't know that much about my father because he died at such a young age, but I do know that he was the man that drove everyone when they had to emigrate, which was a significant job then. Emigration was rife in the fifties in Templenoe and the surrounding areas, and because he had the local hackney car he was the man who brought the emigrants on their journey. That became a feature of life for me later, the amount of people that year after year came back to tell me about those journeys. During the summer they'd come back from all over England and America and appear at the bar. After a drink or two, eventually one of them would say that my dad had driven them to Shannon or down to Cobh for the boat.

And they'd go on and tell me all the details of the journey, telling me all about themselves and their parents crying in the car, looking out the windows at Ireland for the last time as they went. Once they were on the boat or the plane, the parents got back into the car, and then they cried all the way home to Templenoe.

My father would have told me a little about that before he died: the experience of delivering people to the emigrant ship, how sad that was for him. Some of those people went on and made a huge success of their lives, but not all of them. Some of them left Ireland and never saw home again. Maybe that's why emigration has always resonated with me, people leaving home and families being broken up, the countryside becoming deserted and the breaking of communities. It's always struck a chord with me and made me ask why those communities have to be broken up, and what can we do to prevent that.

For my parents it was a tough living. Were they wealthy? Absolutely not. I'd say they just about kept their heads above water, and it didn't become any easier for my mother when my father died, shortly after that All-Ireland final in 1964.

One thing about *The Sunday Game* was that it defined me as a person: to the vast majority of the population I was this person on the television. I only spoke, on average, for a little over three hours per year. Yet, those three or three and a half hours of talking defined me as a person in the eyes of so many people. Perception-wise, I was seen as loudmouthed, outspoken, cranky, negative: I hate this, I hate that.

It's something that bothered me but it was also something that I couldn't do anything about. I suppose we all do it; I certainly do it myself. I watch somebody on television and I like him or don't like him, but the truth is I don't know the person at all.

When you're appearing on *The Sunday Game* you might have a sound bite or two prepared, but not much more than that. On that last day in 2022 I had nothing prepared because it was my final appearance on the programme, but at the end of the game I started crying on television. That wasn't premeditated. At all. I wasn't expecting it. I don't do crying in public. I'll cry, but I'll cry privately and cry quietly. If you don't cry in public you're not going to start by doing it on *The Sunday Game* before about a million people.

It was my last day on *The Sunday Game* but that wasn't why I cried. We had four Templenoe lads winning All-Ireland medals, which was fantastic, but that wasn't it either.

The big thing was family, because family means a lot to me. Contrary to what people think, I'm not that fellow on television, I'm actually a very private person. I don't go to bars at night. Why? Because if there's one drunk on the premises, he marks me for the night. I like to keep very close to family and a few friends, that's it. I rarely go out. We're all very close as a family. Very close. Maybe that's because my father died so young, that the four of us kids bonded together even more, but we've always been very close.

And on that day, seeing my nephews Killian and Adrian win those medals was great, obviously, but the real significance of the day was that those medals were won when Kerry beat Galway. That's because, to the day I die,

Kerry v Galway means only one thing. It was Kerry and Galway who played in an All-Ireland final two days before my father died.

* * *

My father worked hard. He didn't drink, and he was a big strong man who played club football up to 1963, the year before he died, just to keep the club alive. The following year, he was a selector for Kerry when they faced Galway in the All-Ireland senior final. The night before the game, Kerry were staying in the Gresham Hotel on O'Connell Street, and that evening my father had a pain in his chest.

He was out for a walk with one of the players and said as much, and the player said to him, 'Tom, you need to tell the doctor about that.' He refused, because that would have been his way – my father didn't want to miss the game the following day. It would never occur to him not to be on the bench as a selector in Croke Park.

The match was played on Sunday and Galway won. On the Monday night, he came down from Dublin, and on Tuesday night he dropped dead of a massive heart attack.

Because of that, to me, Kerry v Galway has always meant the day my father died. And now I think that the day of the 2022 All-Ireland final was the first-ever time I actually grieved for my father, that I had an opportunity to do so.

I was eight when he died, and I was the eldest. Tommy was the youngest, two years of age, and back then youngsters wouldn't have been brought to funerals. That's not to say I don't have memories of that period. I have very sharp memories of it. I can remember being in the room next to my parents' room, upstairs that Tuesday evening, eight years of age, with Tommy and Mike probably in the room as well. And I can still hear the sound of voices outside the door of the room. To this day, I can hear the thudding of feet walking fast, over and back, and remember not knowing what had happened.

I can't remember my mother ever bringing us together as children to tell us he died, though I do have a vague memory of someone saying the coffin couldn't be brought down the stairs. I think it eventually had to be brought out through the top window of the bar.

The day of the funeral, we weren't brought to the graveyard. We were brought over to the O'Sheas, our neighbours, whose farmhouse overlooked the Templenoe church. I can still remember how it felt, standing up on a rock on the O'Sheas' land, hearing the bell ring as my father's funeral procession left the church. I could see glimpses of the crowd in the churchyard, but that was it. All of that came flooding back to me that day in Croke Park. I don't know if we do grieving that well in Ireland, but we certainly didn't at that time in our history.

I haven't watched that *Sunday Game* clip back. People have asked me if I have, but I've never revisited it because it was a very painful moment. It was a release of whatever had built up over the years.

There were two things about it. First of all, it made people realise who I really was. I wasn't Pat Spillane the outspoken pundit but Pat Spillane the family man, the son who had lost a father.

Since that day, it's amazing the number of people who have come to me and have helped me to piece together everything about my father in the build-up to his death. Pete Hanley was his great friend, and the sub-goalie on that Kerry team. Pete travelled with him over and back to matches and training sessions all the time, and he's told me since that all summer my father had been complaining of pains in the chest but was putting it down to indigestion. Because of that, he was taking Rennies, but obviously it was his heart all the time. He was a very heavy smoker, and the pain on the Saturday night before the All-Ireland final was another warning signal.

On the Monday night, after the final, Pete told me they had gone to a funeral home to say a prayer for the father of Galway captain John Donnellan, who had actually died during the game. They paid their respects and then came down to Killarney. As my father walked over to his car, which was parked in my uncle Jackie Lyne's place, he got another pain in the chest. He leaned against the wall with the pain and it took him a good five minutes before he felt well enough to drive.

Driving home that night, they met a gang of fellows from Sneem whose car had gotten a puncture. They had no jack, and Tom, being the strong man he was, lifted the car to help them replace the tyre, which couldn't have been good for his heart.

On the Tuesday night, he was working in the bar and Jack O'Sullivan Dandy was there with his brother, who was home from England, the last two people left in the place. My father walked out to the yard with Jacko and his brother, said goodnight, and that was it.

So, that *Sunday Game* moment was a special one, and it was probably my moment of bereavement, of release. It was my way of dealing with his death, something that I had never dealt with. And it's amazing that I've learned so much about him from so many people.

He was a wonderful man, but I have very few clear memories of him. I have a faint memory of him playing with Templenoe the year before he died just to make sure Templenoe had 15 fellas out on the field to keep the club alive. He was responsible for developing the pitch below where I live now, and he served as the chairman of the club. I remember he brought me on in 1963 in an U14 game over in Sneem. There were no organised games at that time, but he'd set up a challenge game and brought me on as a sub. I was seven years old and was probably brought on because he was the team manager.

I can remember literally nothing else about him, just what he looked like and that he was a fair and honest man. A great GAA man and a great Templenoe man. A good man. I suppose that his legacy lived on through his sons on the playing fields, and now through his grandsons.

I got a huge reaction after that episode of *The Sunday Game*, not just from people getting to realise what I was really like, but also – and this was probably the biggest reaction – I encountered many other people who had suffered bereavement, particularly the deaths of their fathers. The number of people that I met who said, 'I cried when I was watching you,' and I'd say, 'But I don't know you at all?' That moment touched a raw nerve with a lot of people, and how perhaps they'd never grieved properly, or they'd never enjoyed time with their fathers properly.

His passing meant our world was suddenly turned upside down. My mother was left with a bar, a shop, a couple of petrol pumps, a hackney car and four young kids to rear. No widow's pension, no state assistance of any kind at all. The first thing she did? She sold the car because she couldn't drive.

She reared the four of us and ran the business. That business, when my father died in 1964, was only okay, but in the next 15 to 20 years my mother built it, particularly the bar part, into an absolute success, a huge, huge business that made a lot of money.

She was a great woman. We all like to say of our mothers that they're the greatest mother of all time, but my mother really was. The death of her husband at a young age obviously made her a hard person. I'm not saying that she wasn't a loving person, because she was, but life was hard on her. She lost both of her own parents and both of my father's parents in a very short time, a span of three years in the early sixties, so life had already been very hard on her. She never complained, though. She just got on with it. She never showed emotion. Did I ever see her crying in front of me? No. I told someone that Mam never gave out to us, which she never did – but she didn't have to, because she had 'the look'. And that look was enough for her.

But she spoiled us and because I was the eldest I was particularly spoiled. My wife, Rosarii, recently reminded me of all the bad habits that she inherited because of what my mother did for me. An example? My mother didn't just clean my football boots, she polished them. The woman was trying to run a business, but three big galoots – me, Mike and Tom – would come in from training and my mother would take the boots, wash the boots, clean the boots, polish the boots. She'd wash all our gear, dry and iron it, and put all our gear out, with the holy water sprinkled on it, for games.

During the summer when we'd be training for Kerry, all through the seventies and eighties, we would be sleeping in until one o'clock or two o'clock to get rest for training or for a game. So, when my mother handed me over – reluctantly – to Rosarii, those were part of the instructions. For instance, I never cooked in my life, so Rosarii had to do all the cooking as well.

Clearly, she gave us bad habits. Like a lot of other people learning to drive, I tipped and dented the car a few times. I'd have to explain to her that there was a panel scratched or a bonnet busted. You know what she'd always say? Cars can be replaced. She never gave out. Even if I was in the wrong, her philosophy stayed constant: cars can be replaced.

But Mam didn't do hugs. She wasn't one for wishing the best of luck in games. There was little outward display of affection, but she was our rock. Mam parked her life to raise us, and because there were four kids depending on her and on the business, she looked after herself. She fed herself well and was a woman of faith. She knelt at the kitchen table after she locked up the bar and brushed and polished and washed the place. At one o'clock every morning, Mam would be kneeling on the chair at the end of the table saying a full half an hour of prayers.

She worked hard. Never took a day off. Never had staff. Never complained. Ever. Because of that, she never saw us playing football in her life, even as youngsters, and the football pitch in Templenoe is only half a mile away from the house. No distance at all. But she never, ever went to the football field to see us. She watched us if the games were on television in the latter years, but did she wish us luck before the game? Nope. Did she say well done after the game? Nope. She blessed us with holy water on the way out to the game, and all she'd say was 'Just remember who you are.'

I remember the only time she changed her message. You'd have to have a handle on the local rivalries in Kerry to appreciate it. My mother was from the Legion club in Killarney, because she was part of the Lyne dynasty, and their arch rivals were, and are, Dr Crokes. Always.

The only time – and I mean the only time – my mother ever came into our bedroom the morning of a game was the morning Kenmare District played Dr Crokes in the Kerry county final. She said, 'Do this for me.' And the following morning, after we'd beaten Crokes, she came in and hugged us. That was one of the few times we got a hug.

She worked every day in the bar but a door opened from there into the kitchen, so when she cooked she'd have the door open. If somebody wanted a drink, she went through to the bar from the kitchen. She had her own dinner and supper at the kitchen table with the door open. From the time when we were able to do anything at all, we were behind that bar, so from nine or ten years of age, we were working there as well.

And she ran a great bar. In those days, the early to mid-sixties, there was no such thing as tourism as we understand it now. In terms of trade, there was one church nearby, so

Sunday was a big day for the bar, but it was just the local population. Maybe one or two people came out from Kenmare the odd time, but that was about it.

She was a very decent woman. When it came to Christmas, there were a lot of big families in the area, and that meant a lot of struggling families. From the late fifties and into the sixties, the area would have been fairly impoverished, and when it came to Christmas and the Christmas box, my mother would put half as much again into the order: food and drink, free, gratis, for people with big families.

She had a book at one stage and there were a lot of people on tick using that book, but there were a lot of people who never paid – never paid to this day. She didn't chase them down. With funerals, and the free bar for a couple of hours afterwards, there were many times she wasn't paid. Did she ever go looking for payment? No. That was my mother – kind, caring and generous.

There were old people in the area living on their own, and she looked after them – and she did it because she wanted to do it. Every day without fail, I'd be sent over to an old woman nearby delivering dinner for her made by my mother.

Johnny Bán O'Sullivan was our best customer, one of those fellas who came to the bar every night and who had his own stool. He was my mother's best friend. She'd send up dinner to Johnny, and she'd send us to town to get his messages for him.

People can talk about bars, and we've lost so many of them now, but the bar at that time was the community centre. It was the focal point. Spillane's, with the bar and the shop and the petrol pumps, was the hub of the community, and she made sure she looked after the people in that community.

* * *

The big day was always the 15th of August because that was the pattern day in Kenmare, the feast day that's also a gathering day of all the emigrants. They'd all be home for the 15th of August.

It was also the day we dreaded because it was the one day, invariably, that from six or seven o'clock on, there'd be a fight. Or two or three. It was terrible. I remember, as a ten-year-old, standing with my mother as she separated two fighting farmers. That was a regular occurrence. She was a brave woman and she never backed away from them, but their carry-on was selfish. I can see now how horrible it was, and because of rows like that, the 15th was a day we never looked forward to. These were arguments that were like two bald men fighting over a comb – 'Hold me back' and all that. But my mother would be the one standing there in the middle of two big old galoots who should have known a lot better.

The other fair days were good days but those were days for fighting as well, because people didn't come out that often. The farmers only came out for the fair days once a month, and the cattle buyers came once a month, so they wouldn't be that used to drinking. Because of that, every cattle fair had a row of some description. The sheep fairs were probably worse again, because they were even rarer. The sheep men weren't drinking twelve times a year like the cattle men and were even less used to alcohol.

Christmas was amazing because that was our next big time. That was when the immigrants came home and, Jesus, they drank and they drank and they drank.

* * *

One of the most famous people in Ireland at that time in the sixties was a big industrialist, Jefferson Smurfit senior, who had a house in Rossdohan, near Tahilla, just ten miles back the road from us. He and his partner were great customers of my mother's, and they'd drive down from Dublin and stop in my mother's for an hour or two's drinking, then get a box filled with whiskey and beer and whatever.

I was the petrol pump attendant and can remember him arriving in the purple Rolls-Royce, which had two tanks in it. At that time, the petrol pump went as far as 10 pounds. So, if you had a car that was taking over 10 pounds (there weren't many of those at the time, except for Jefferson's purple Rolls-Royce) you went with the pump as far as 9 pounds 11 shillings and 11 pence, then stopped and started again. To fill the two tanks of Jefferson Smurfit's Rolls Royce was about 11 pounds in the late sixties.

I remember another number from that time. He said to my mother one time, 'If you have any money to spare, Mrs Spillane, you should maybe invest in my company.' Sadly, she didn't. I remember reading afterwards that if you had £5,000 invested with Smurfit at that time, 20 years later it would have been worth half a million. There you go.

* * *

In the late sixties, the English tourists started to come. We got a great calibre of tourists. A lot of them came to the Great Southern and Parknasilla hotels nearby, and my mother had loyal English tourists who'd visit every year, and they were the kind of tourist that, whatever amount of money they brought with them, they spent every penny of it before they headed home. They had a pre-lunch drink, a pre-dinner drink, drink during dinner, after dinner, all evening. They were really good people and she nurtured that trade. She was very, very popular and she ran a good pub – but no after-hours.

By 1969, nine in ten cars passing by were GB-registered. Unfortunately, when the Troubles broke out, that finished more or less overnight. That was disappointing, but she never complained.

There were other tests. At one point, two guards came out two or three nights a week and parked a squad car behind the bar. They'd go into the kitchen and drink eight or nine pints while my mother would be up and down bringing pints to them, at no charge, as well as looking after the customers out in the bar. In later years, I asked her if they were taking advantage of her, but she said they were protecting her. That was the climate at the time: she thought they were doing a great job. I thought they were just hungry freeloaders.

* * *

When eventually my mother did retire, she retired back to our house. That was progress. In retirement, arthritis hit her, not surprisingly, given she had been 40 years on her feet, but in her eighties, she got her knee replaced and never looked back. My sister Margaret minded her in the latter years, and when I used to come home from teaching I'd visit her in Margaret's house over in Kenmare. For the last year or two, there was a certain amount of dementia. She'd know you one day, and she wouldn't know you another, but one day I arrived in and it looked like she was dead.

Myself and my brother-in-law were there, and we didn't know how to work out for sure if she was dead. We ended up taking out a mirror to try to see her breath but that didn't work either. We couldn't figure it out even when we rang my sister, who's a nurse, for advice. Mam would have laughed away at us – two eejits.

That day I did something that I'd never done before. It came back to me that I'd heard, somewhere along the line, that the sense of hearing is the last thing to go in a person who's dying. I remember sitting by the bed, and I held her by the hand and said, 'Mam, I love you.' I don't think I had ever said that before to her, but it hit home: she was gone, after all she had done for us.

∗ ∗ ∗

After the 1984 or 1985 All-Ireland, I came home with my fourth or fifth All-Ireland medal and a man of the match award under my arm. I should have been back in Templenoe on the Monday night, and when I landed in the door at about seven o'clock on a Wednesday, I was fairly full of the joys. Instead of giving me a hug and congratulating me and saying how proud she was, she just said, 'You should be home on Monday night, get down to the bar now.' Winning All-Irelands, working full-time – but still on duty in the bar.

That's the great thing about Kerry and the great thing about my mother. She kept you grounded. 'Remember who you are' was always the last message. Until the day I die, that's her message to me, and it has carried me through life. That's the legacy of my mother. That's who she was, straight down the line.

Her influence remains with me. The way she conducted herself with us as a family but also within the bar, with regular and occasional customers alike, and above all with the community in Templenoe.

CHAPTER 2

TEMPLENOE: THE HOME PLACE

How to describe Templenoe?

As you travel the country, you'll often see the sign 'Drive Slow Through Village'. Someone amended the one near Templenoe: 'Drive Slow (or you'll miss the) Village'.

Templenoe is a narrow coastal area between the Macgillycuddy's Reeks and Kenmare Bay, stretching from just outside Kenmare to Blackwater Bridge. There's a big hinterland behind it heading up towards the mountains, but that's very sparsely populated. It's a beautiful scenic area with the Reeks on one side and beaches on the other, and the people of the area are lovely, straightforward, honest and hard-working.

Nearby is Dromore Castle, which was the home of the O'Mahonys. Harold Sigerson O'Mahony from Dromore

Castle was the winner of a Wimbledon title and of an Olympic medal in tennis. The O'Mahonys were different people: in the Church of Ireland graveyard here, all the headstones are facing east except for the main headstone of the O'Mahonys, which is facing west. An O'Mahony had always to be buried facing over their estate. Harold probably put us on the map as a tennis champion, though legend has it he came to a bad end after a day's drinking in Glencar, but that's another story.

Templenoe might never have figured too prominently on any maps, but it's a typical rural area on the western seaboard of Ireland, a peripheral location on that seaboard. There's no village, no employment as such. What do we have at the moment? We have a shop, a pub and two churches, but as of July 2023, the churches closed for mass.

In the sixties, the Templenoe GAA catchment area, to put it that way, had five national schools. But in the last 20 years, nothing. Only for the GAA club, Templenoe wouldn't have an identity, Templenoe wouldn't have a future and Templenoe wouldn't have something to live for.

It annoys me when I hear people say rural Ireland is doing well now. Rural Ireland in certain areas is doing very well. Rural Ireland close to the big cities and big towns is doing well; elsewhere rural Ireland is struggling because there are no jobs, no employment, and the young people are leaving. Templenoe is a good example of that.

I've always said that GAA clubs don't get the credit they deserve. The GAA club everywhere – but particularly in rural Ireland – is the glue that keeps communities together. The GAA's manifesto sums it up well.

We all belong here. In this place. At this time. We belong not because of who we are or where we come from. Being here means belonging. Belonging means knowing you're part of a community, a community that has a place for all. Where potential is nurtured, where individuals become teams who honour the legacy of those who went before and strive to build a legacy of their own.

Some of us play. Some of us used to play. Some of us never played. We all belong. Belonging means having a voice, means being able to say what you think is right, being listened to.

Belonging means respecting each other, means being there for each other on the pitch. Off the pitch. Belonging means rolling our sleeves up and doing what needs to be done. We all belong, whether it's our first day or our hundredth year. We all belong here because this place belongs to us all. Our GAA. Where we all belong.

Add in the old AIB quote 'You don't choose your club, you inherit it', and even if you're not a GAA person, you get the idea. It's about identity. Charles Kickham made Knocknagow and the honour of the little village famous. That's Templenoe too, a GAA club maintained and driven by families who pass the love of the GAA from one generation to the next. But at underage level, we have to amalgamate with other places nearby, like many other clubs.

We're lucky that we have a senior team. We went to the senior club final in Kerry in 2022, which was a fantastic achievement. Will we be a senior club team in 20 years' time? Or in 10 years' time? Probably not, because for little areas it's cyclical – it's about population first and foremost. At underage level for U14, U15 and U16, we amalgamate with Tuosist, Sneem and Derrynane. If you go from Tuosist into Kenmare, it's 20 miles. From Kenmare to the end of Derrynane, it's another 20 miles. So that's a 40-mile journey to get one team at each age group, and that's the reality of a lot of places all over rural Ireland. When you take a step back, it means that south Kerry, an area almost the size of County Louth, is producing one team to play U17 – and playing 13-a-side at that. The GAA club is always the barometer. The canary in the coal mine. Where you see a GAA club struggling to field a team or amalgamating with neighbours to field a team, you know an area is in trouble.

But Templenoe is just a great area. It's an area of small farmers, an area that the young have always had to leave to get work. But it's a place with good people who never let you rise above your station, good people that keep you grounded, and I think the GAA club has a lot to do with it. It put Templenoe on the map, and so did the Spillane brothers years ago. Now it's on the map with my nephews, and Tadhg Morley, and Gavin Crowley.

That's important. When you come from such a tiny area in Ireland, particularly in the peripheral regions, the automatic thing when you're asked where you're from is to name the biggest town near you and say you're from that area. But we can say we're from Templenoe and know that people have heard of it, and we're proud of that.

The late Paudie Palmer, the GAA commentator with County Sound in Cork, was a Templenoe man and a good friend of mine. He always tells people that we brought Sam Maguire eight times to Templenoe but that there was never a bonfire lit when the cup was brought, because you do it and get on with it.

Are there any statues or plaques or any fields named after us? Have we ever been recognised for our achievements? No, but that's just the way – you shrug the shoulders, keep the head down and keep it going. But at least we can say in our own different ways that we helped Templenoe in some way and we're proud to be from here.

Templenoe wasn't a successful club, but if there was a prize for socialising, we'd have won the county title every year. It's a cliché, but there's a reason it's a cliché: it's true.

The club is where you're with the lads you grew up with, the lads you went to school with – the GAA club is a full cradle-to-grave service. The lads you're with when you make your first communion will be there in the guard of honour when you're being laid to rest.

I didn't have a lot of close friends on the Kerry team I played with, because Kerry's such a big county, and everyone is spread so far apart. Killarney is the nearest big town and there was no one from Killarney on our team, so it was an hour and a quarter up the road to the Tralee gang, two hours to Páidí Ó Sé out west, and so on.

That meant that after a Munster final in Killarney, I was in Charlie Foley's with the Templenoe lads or, in Cork, down in the Imperial with the Templenoe lads or, after an All-Ireland final, in McGovern's or the Cat and Cage in Dublin with the Templenoe lads. They're my friends.

People often mention Kerry victories to me, but the club victories meant more to me, in all honesty. That's because of the relationship our family had with the club for decades. My father helped to get the club's first pitch and was chairman eventually, and in time I was chairman myself.

The monthly meeting of the club was always held in the kitchen of the pub, so from the time I was knee-high to a grasshopper I was around the meetings, listening to what was going on. The AGMs could have a touch of Mrs Doyle in *Father Ted* about them. There was a certain amount of 'go on, go on, go on' when it came to the various jobs in the club, and it only ever became mildly contentious when it came to choosing selectors for the Kerry teams. Even then, Templenoe had a simple rule of thumb when it came time to vote: we always voted for the selector who lived closest to us on the basis that he might look after the Templenoe lads. Not that he might be the best football brain for the sake of the county, but he might be the best option for us. One night, that debate became very technical, and there was a sudden outbreak of geography when a debate got stuck on which was closest to us: Brosna or Lispole. Google Maps would have come in very handy that evening.

I was secretary of Templenoe long before becoming chairman, all the way back in 1978 and 1979. (In those years, while I was sorting out club registrations, I also won two All-Ireland medals, two All-Stars and a Footballer of the Year award.)

I organised tours of London while I was secretary. One particular memory is of our bus breaking down in Knightsbridge, outside Harrods. There's a photograph somewhere of the lot of us pushing this bus, which has a banner draped over it: 'Templenoe Football Tour of London'. Harrods is clearly visible in the background.

On that tour, we played a game on a pitch just outside Wormwood Scrubs, and the inmates took a great interest in the game. Or an interest in shouting at us, at least.

'Go home, Paddy, someone's screwing your wife,' and so on.

'Whoever it is, it's not you, you bollocks,' was the usual response.

When I retired from playing, my 30 years with *The Sunday Game* meant I couldn't give the commitment to train a team full-time. I trained juveniles, but that was a mistake, particularly when my son Pat was involved. I was too loud, too caught up in the whole thing. Once, as part of a check-up, I was put on a blood pressure monitor for 24 hours. When the nurse checked the reading she said, 'For 23 hours, your blood pressure was perfect, but between 7 and 8 yesterday it was very high.' I was training the Templenoe U12s for that hour. That was the spike in blood pressure.

When I became chairman of Templenoe, I learned about a different kind of pressure, one GAA club officers everywhere are familiar with: fundraising. The irony is that I should have been better at that, because the best example of all time, the greatest networker I ever met, was one of my best friends: Páidí Ó Sé.

If you were with a crowd of fellas at a bar counter, Páidí would come over and tap you on the shoulder and say it straight out: 'Is there anyone here I should know?' As a networker he couldn't be beaten. Never missed an opportunity. The greatest example of that was the U2 meeting. The two of us were in a restaurant in Dublin, having dinner with a man who was fairly well-connected himself, when Páidí spotted his prey at a far table.

'Look,' he said. 'Bono and The Edge. I'd love to meet them.'

The man we were with – who shall remain nameless – knew Bono to say hello to, so he said he'd make the effort, anyway. He went over to the lads' table. After a minute, he looked back at our table and nodded. Páidí was over like a shot with the hand out, 'How are you doing?'

When the pleasantries were over, Páidí arrived back at our table. I could see his mind ticking away still, though, and eventually he piped up again to our go-between: 'Would there be any chance of a photo with the two lads, do you think?'

Our man groaned. 'Ah, I don't know, Páidí, that might be going a bit far. And anyway, we've no camera.'

This was before smartphones, so we were stuck. Until Páidí solved the problem by hurling out of the restaurant and coming back with a camera.

To be fair to Bono and The Edge, when our man went back again to see if there was any chance of a snap, they said 'No bother' and came and stood in with Páidí for the picture.

I was looking on, shaking my head, when I heard Páidí: 'Listen, lads, if ye ever come down to west Kerry call into the pub, we're in Ventry …'

'We will, we will,' said Bono, who was clearly on his way out the door for home at this stage of the evening.

'Look,' said Páidí, 'why don't you give me your number there and I'll let you know when I'm home if you want to call in?'

I then heard Bono say, 'Yeah, it's 087 …' and he was gone.

Páidí then sat down to finish his dinner, having met Bono and The Edge, having gotten them into a photograph to be put behind the counter of his bar, and having tapped Bono's mobile number into his own phone for some point in the future when it might come in handy.

At times over the years, I thought the likes of Colm O'Rourke was a good networker. One of his teammates said one time that he'd slagged him: 'Rourkey, aren't you lucky that all your pals are multimillionaires?' But he was in the ha'penny place compared to Páidí. Nobody could network like him. I certainly couldn't.

* * *

When Catriona McKiernan was running in the London Marathon one time, and going for the world record, I was sent a cutting from an English newspaper which described a press conference she gave beforehand. She was asked who the sportsperson she most admired was, and she gave my name.

The man who sent me the cutting was Arthur Ryan, the head of Penneys in Ireland, and we became friends. We'd meet in the Berkeley Court regularly, and his vision for the business used to amaze me. If I met him on a Saturday evening in the Berkeley Court, he'd have visited four of his stores that day and walked around for an hour in each one, observing what was going on. The reason I mention him is that when Templenoe got their first set of sponsored jerseys, Penneys sponsored them. He was my sole networking contact. I was chairman of Templenoe by then, in the early 2000s, because I wanted to give something back.

We were struggling. We had a pitch with sheep grazing on rushes in the middle of it, with bad drainage, and I felt embarrassed by that. I wanted to do something about it.

I had some great people with me, which is always the key if you become chairman of a club. We were struggling at underage, so we set up a Bord na nÓg within the club that would bear fruit eventually with the senior team we have now, and we started fundraising to develop the pitch. We put in a stand and installed floodlights and eventually got a second field.

The fundraising we approached in two ways. We decided we wouldn't sell tickets or go door-to-door to collect money; we'd organise a system where you'd become a patron of the club for €1,000 – but you could do so as an individual, a family or a group of families. Or you could become a sponsor for €500.

At the monthly meetings, I'd read out the names: 'Johnny Murphy became a patron this week …' and I'd say we ended up shaming a lot of people into becoming patrons.

We also had Jackie Healy-Rae holding the government to ransom at the time, so our timing was good. And he became a patron of the club himself for €1,000, good going for a Kilgarvan man. Jackie was instrumental in getting us lots of Lotto grants. We had a meeting once with the then sports minister, Jim McDaid, which Jackie brokered, and we got a grant of €50,000 out of it.

We got a second grant afterwards, which was great, but to top it all we went looking for a third grant, which was unheard of. What encouraged us was that our constituency had the man holding up the government (Jackie) back the road, and it also had the man who was sports minister (John O'Donoghue, who succeeded Jim McDaid) a bit further back the road.

I went to see them, and they were both doubtful about a third grant but gave the classic politician's answer: 'I'll see what I can do.'

When the grants were eventually announced Jackie rang me to say, 'God, this was the toughest of all time – but I've secured a grant for ye, tough as it was.'

A half-hour later, one of John O'Donoghue's officials rang with an oddly familiar message: 'This was a tough ask, but you'll be delighted to hear that the grant was approved for such and such an amount.'

'That's great,' I said, 'but Jackie Healy-Rae was on to me half an hour ago and he gave me a different figure.'

'It couldn't be,' said the official. 'Our department is the one that gives out the money.'

'I'll ring Jackie back,' I said to him. And I did: 'Is that figure right?'

Jackie's story was this: 'I asked Minister O'Donoghue in the Chamber what the man in Templenoe was going to get, and he showed me the figure. I said that figure would disappoint all the great people of Templenoe, but he said that was all that was on offer.

'I left the Chamber and went upstairs to see the man himself in his office. The door was ajar and he was on the phone, but I shouted in to him, "The great man in Templenoe will be disappointed with the amount he's getting."

'And the man in the office said, "Would he take another thirty thousand?"

'"He would."'

And that's how we got the third grant. On the basis of shouting in the door of an office in Government Buildings.

If I have to explain exactly who 'the man in the office' was, then I'm afraid you're reading the wrong book, but suffice to say he was clearly very important.

✱ ✱ ✱

We opened the pitch in 2003 with a game between Kerry and Dublin, thanks to my friends Páidí and Tommy Lyons, who were managing the two teams. Bertie Ahern came down to open it officially for us. It was the week that news broke about Bertie splitting with Celia Larkin, so there was huge press coverage of him and, by extension, our pitch opening.

I've never been involved with the club since because I gave so much of myself in the seven years I was chairman. The day after the opening, I was fatigued, having been on the go for so long, organising everything. I went to the doctor and he examined me.

'There's only one thing for it,' he said. 'A shot of morphine.'

The only problem was I had to drive back out the road after and I hit a wall on the way home, though no one was hurt, thank God. When I walked in the door, Rosarii said the eyes were rolling around in my head. She sent me to bed, and I was there for two days recovering.

One night, in the middle of fundraising and organising, I came home from the club's monthly meeting. At it, I had announced we had gotten a Lotto grant, we'd been granted planning permission for a 350-person stand and owner-ship of the second pitch had finally been secured. I announced those three things, and I was pissed off that there wasn't more made of the news. I couldn't think of another club chairman in Ireland who would announce three bits of good news like that without hearing some applause at least.

When I got home I was complaining to Rosarii about the reaction, and she asked me an obvious question: 'Why do you do it?'

And I said, 'I do it because I want to do it.'

And that brought it home to me – that's what the club is all about. I wanted to do it and that's what drove me to do it. To keep it going, like Clifford said.

✳ ✳ ✳

I played for Templenoe from the age of 15 to 39, a good quarter of a century. I ended up with the Templenoe Bs, and if my knee hadn't given way, I'd still be trying to play now. Playing and training for Templenoe was my high. I didn't take drugs, but that was my drug. We won a junior county title in 1974 and a novice county title in 1975, though we were beaten in an intermediate final. We usually flitted between divisions two and five.

We always struggled for numbers, and at underage we often had to slip in one or two overage players. That brought its own challenges because the overage player would be given his younger brother's name as a temporary identity, which led to confusion when you were calling someone for a pass.

Foreigners sometimes made up the numbers for us and were welcome. Dutch, Germans, South Africans, Americans, English – they all wore the blue and white of Templenoe.

Early on a few Dutch people who settled in the area in the seventies helped us fill out teams. Henk Bons came on for us against Lispole one day and said to me when he ran onto the field, 'I'm on at corner forward, Pat, where's that?'

'Come in here alongside me, Henk.'

He's still in Templenoe. Still part of the club. When we played in the All-Ireland junior championship quarter-final in Birmingham against John Mitchels a couple of years back, Hank volunteered his big Range Rover to bring across all the gear for the players. We packed it all in and that saved us money on the plane.

We kept it going alright, even during the bad years, which was one of the reasons I was so proud last year to see four Templenoe lads win All-Ireland senior medals. When it comes to describing what the club and Templenoe mean to me, I struggle, really, because it's so deep. It's part of my DNA. It's where I was born, where I've lived all my life and where I want to be buried. That sense of identity has always stood to me, no matter where I've been or what I've encountered. It was certainly a huge help in my first spell living away from home as a raw child.

CHAPTER 3

LIVING NEXT DOOR TO THE BISHOP

When I left home at 12 years of age, it was to head for St Brendan's College as a boarder. The role the school (also known as The Sem) played in my life – as a footballer, as a teacher – was huge, and that came down to a big decision my mother made.

If the three of us had stayed home, working in the bar in the evening and doing a bit of school when it could be fitted in, it wasn't going to work out. Hence her decision, and her sacrifice, to send me and my brothers away to St Brendan's. She kept my sister Margaret, who was much younger than us, at home, so it was a sacrifice for her as well, staying at home.

That first night in St Brendan's was tough, though, and not just for me. My mother told me later that the night she left me in St Brendan's was the lowest she felt since my father died – the one time she had cried since that day.

In those days, you went in in September and you only came home in November, December and at Easter, so you were abandoned. There were visits allowed at the weekend, but my mother didn't have a car so she couldn't visit. For three months you were stuck in a big, lonely building in Killarney. Our accommodation was called the 'new' dormitory, and there would have been about 60 First Years crying all night. That went on for weeks – the crying, the bed-wetting, the wailing.

Boarding school is sink or swim. I cried as much as anyone else that first night. The second night I didn't cry quite as much, but I didn't sleep. I looked up at the ceiling for the night. But the day after that, we got out onto the football field. Fr Pearse was training us.

Paradise.

From then on, there were no problems for me.

The field across from the seminary became my place of pilgrimage for five years, every day after school at a quarter to four. It set the tone for how I looked at football. It became my obsession. Every day I trained, and by 'trained' I mean kicking and kicking and kicking.

Bear in mind that there were no real underage competitions at that time, so kids wouldn't have come through years and years of competitive games. This was the first time we had organised games. I realised, 'Wait, I'm as good as these fellas.' I got good coaching and plenty of practice, and it was bound to have an effect.

That 'new' dormitory was attached to the Bishop's Palace, which meant that every evening we saw a flash car zoom up the long drive to the palace door: Bishop Eamonn Casey. Little did we know that next door to us he was entertaining Annie Murphy with some of the greatest shenanigans in Irish religious history.

His driving made little impression on us. For me, school was all about the football and the three and a half hours of compulsory study every night. It was good for me because it showed me how to work hard. Anything I ever achieved in life was because of the hard slog I put in, and I didn't waste those compulsory study sessions.

For all those reasons, boarding school was perfect for me. It wasn't a great experience if you were shy or introverted, probably, and while we've all heard a lot about the religious orders' abuse of children in various institutions, I never saw anything like that. It might have been going on, but I never saw it.

St Brendan's also helped my fitness for football in another way: the race for food. Getting from the dormitory or the classroom to the refectory was a matter of urgency, because the first man to the table got the best of the food. The sprint down the corridor was crucial. I could anticipate the bell, and soon I worked out that the stairs could be negotiated if you jumped from one flight to another rather than actually taking the steps. Two ten-foot jumps, and I wasn't beaten that often at all to the food.

The first year I was in school was also the first time St Brendan's won the All-Ireland senior football colleges title, and that made an impression on me and the other First Years. The way these players were treated around the school – they were like demi-gods. John O'Keeffe was the star of that team – big, strong, the best player. He was the Tom Brady of the side. They got special meals and had those at different times, so you knew they were a breed apart. Naturally enough, you wanted to be one of them when your own time came.

There were other motivations too. When St Brendan's would play an away game, even in Tralee, a train would be chartered for the whole school to go. Cork, Limerick, wherever – we'd all pile into it. The team had their own carriage. But in the old trains, there were compartments, and because the Sem had a big female following with the girls' schools in Killarney – the Loreto, the Presentation, the Mercy – on the way back home if you slipped into the players' carriage, the compartments might have the lights out and the curtains drawn. A First Year could see that these were more of the fruits of victory.

* * *

I got a scholarship after First Year for being the most improved student. That wasn't hard given the base I was starting from – I was probably the worst student there arriving into First Year but I had improved on the back of the work I put in.

There were other scholarships on offer as well. There were island scholarships for lads from Valentia, for instance, and we used to look up to them. You might hear, 'Such and such came third in the island scholarship exam,' but eventually someone asked just how many boys were taking the island scholarship exam in the first place. Four.

When we got older and played for the school ourselves, we had great battles with the likes of Coláiste Chríost Rí from Cork, who were basically Nemo Rangers to us. They'd give you a lesson because even if we had a team that was better on the basic skills, Chríost Rí always had that bit of cuteness, those smarts that got them over the line. They were always very good.

Tralee CBS were good at that time too, with a great forward from Austin Stacks – Mikey Sheehy. I captained St Brendan's one year and he was the Tralee captain, and we would have known all about him: he was outstanding.

In Fifth Year, we got to an All-Ireland colleges final against St Patrick's College of Cavan, which was obviously a big deal. The night before we stayed in the Spa Hotel in Lucan and went to the Phoenix Park the morning of the game to work out a tactic for the throw-in.

In fairness, the tactic worked, and we got a point from it, but for the rest of the game we hardly threatened their goal. St Pat's were an anomaly because there was no age limit and in the Ulster colleges competition they stayed on an extra year. In real terms it meant you had sixteen-year-olds playing against nineteen-year-olds, which is no contest. They gave us a lesson, and at half-time I was taken off. I was desperate. If someone at that match had said that lad will win a lot of All-Ireland medals, he'd have been locked up.

* * *

Early on in First Year, I made pals with another boarder, a fella who was all the way from beyond Dingle: Páidí Ó Sé. Even then, he was a rogue and you knew he was a rogue, but he was a lovable rogue. We were similar enough in that our fathers were dead but our mothers worshipped us and both made sure we got everything we wanted.

In 1972, as Fifth Years, we were left out of the Sem to go to the All-Ireland final, Kerry versus Offaly, the two of us. We got permission from our mothers and hit for Dublin on the train that morning. We went to Croke Park, but Kerry were beaten.

We had a couple of hours to kill before the train home, but we ran into a few lads from Páidí's neck of the woods. Even then, Páidí was more advanced than most of us, so he said we'd have a drink. One thing led to another, and we missed the train, though we did make it to a dance later in the evening in Mountjoy Square. Afterwards, the west Kerry lads were heading for a house off Clonliffe Road, so we walked back that way around 2 a.m.

As we did, we noticed the gates of Croke Park were open, so we went in, the two of us. The stadium was completely empty, but after our night out we were running around pretending to kick an imaginary ball over the bar. Innocent out. Little did we know that we'd win an All-Ireland there three years later. There was consternation in the Sem, of course, with no trace of us Sunday night or Monday morning, but we got home eventually. And we weren't even punished, to be honest. Our status as footballers saved us.

Unfortunately, Páidí didn't last too much longer in the school. An Ghaeltacht were planning a football tour of London and he got permission to go, which made us green with envy. He didn't spare us before he headed off either, telling us of the wild adventures that lay ahead.

The night he came back, we all assembled in his cubicle and he unveiled a vast array of magazines that he had picked up in London, which almost floored us, innocents that we were. Sadly, word got out that Páidí had brought back a treasure trove, and soon afterwards his cubicle was searched and the contraband found. He got expelled and moved up to Listowel, settling in with his brother, but that wasn't the last I saw of him.

My football career owes a huge amount to St Brendan's. Fr Pearse and Fr Linnane were big figures in football in the school, as was Jim Hegarty, who sent me a lovely card when I finished up with *The Sunday Game*. They were good coaches – not authoritarian but encouraging and fair, and we responded. Their attitude was one of *mol an óige*, and I brought that into teaching myself when I qualified. To do so, I headed north to Limerick. It was a different dynamic to landing at St Brendan's. I had the experience of years of boarding school, which helped me to settle in college. I also had the benefit of years of good football coaching, which helped me to settle with Kerry.

CHAPTER 4

STOPPING THE ALL BLACKS IN THEIR TRACKS

I was in the second cohort of PE teachers to start full-time in Thomond College. There was a third year when I started, but they had begun their studies over in England, in Strawberry Hill.

The batch immediately in front of me had begun their training in the Brandon Hotel in Tralee because the college facilities in Limerick weren't yet ready – that would be the late Brian Mullins and his group, who were second years when I went in. So, we were the second full year of PE teachers to go to the National College of Physical Education. Hand on heart, can I say that fitness and PE have improved in this country over the five decades since?

Not a hope in the world, but I'll come back to that.

PE college was great for me. I loved it – it was a sports college, you were learning to play all the different sports, and we had wonderful times. Were we prepared for teaching? We were the first of our kind to go out and do teaching practice, which was good. We did teaching practice in national schools in Limerick, which presumably was to ease us into teaching by starting us with younger classes. Then I did a couple of months teaching practice in Tralee. I also spent two months in Coláiste Dhúlaigh, Coolock, which had no facilities and was an eye-opener. That prepared us for what real-life teaching was.

Did what we learned in the National College of Physical Education – the courses, the lectures, the theory – help? Not at all. One issue was that a lot of the lecturers were English and hadn't a clue about the Irish education system. And a lot of those lecturers just didn't like us at all.

I never forgot one horrible bastard who coached rugby. On a Friday morning we'd do swimming first, and the second class was rugby. He always insisted on clean yellow socks, white togs and a blue top – even in the winter months. And the first thing the bastard used to make us do when we'd go out was to roll on the ground – just to demean us and make us feel like dirt.

There was a lot of that, particularly from those English lecturers. Looking back, I wouldn't say a lot of them were good lecturers. There was another bad bastard, who's dead since, a lecturer in physiology who took a keen interest in the students' bodies.

Was I sexually abused? No, I wasn't. But this bastard took a particular 'liking' to me from the day I went for the first interview to get into the college. Dr Watson was his name, and when he was teaching he liked to bring you down the basement, where his lab was, to do his tests. The door would have to be locked when this guy was doing his tests.

He had a particular fondness for checking to see whether you'd ruptured your groin, and he was also big into measuring body percentage fats with callipers and other instruments. It was scary, but when you were trying to get in to the college you were going along with it.

Were people caught by him? I wouldn't be surprised. Was I caught? No, because I'd freeze, make myself motionless, or jump. But I'll never forget all the mornings that I was down there in that lab, and all the body fat tests, and, 'Oh, I must check to see did you rupture your groin.' Was it a form of grooming? Perhaps it was. In any case, it didn't go any further.

The National College of Physical Education was a small college, so we all knew each other, staff and students. After my final exams, another lecturer, who was a friend of mine, said to me, 'Three or four of your final papers have been handed in, and parts of your answers are missing. In some cases, it wasn't the last page of the answer but the second last or third last page of an answer.' And it suddenly dawned on me that for those final exams I had handed my papers up to this Dr Watson.

In fairness to the college, they gave me the benefit of the doubt. In effect they said, 'Look, if you have the last page, then something must have happened in between.'

That lecturer was a bad bastard, but generally as students we had a great time, an absolutely great time. Because it was football, football, football.

* * *

When you talk about the evolution of Gaelic football, and of modern-day Gaelic football in particular, a lot of it emanated from the National College of Physical Education because you were now producing guys who knew about fitness, knew about physiology and the workings of the body, knew about weights, knew about video analysis.

We were the first graduates to bring that knowledge onto the football field, but later there came a stage when most of the county managers were graduates of the NCPE. You'd have to ask, what did they bring to the Gaelic football scene when they came out of college? I'd say the fact that they introduced cones in their hundreds to training sessions is about the limit of it.

At that stage, in the seventies, we were doing video analysis of our games with Thomond as a matter of course, and at the same time we won an All-Ireland club title and went two years without being beaten.

The Thomond footballers were training one day when New Zealand were in town to play Munster. We trained on the opposite pitch to them, as a kind of 'Fuck ye, we're the GAA club'. While we were at it, the All Blacks stopped their own training session to come over and watch us.

Larry McCarthy started with me as a first year, and he was Mr GAA. He organised the buses, he looked after the player registrations, he got the laundry done, got the footballs, handled the grant from the college and was the goalkeeper on our freshers' football team.

He was also the goalkeeper on our freshers' hurling team, which was the worst hurling team ever seen. We had the bare 15 players, and I often said my last hurling game was for the Thomond College freshers, where I was full-forward against St Patrick's College, Drumcondra. I was marking Brian Cody, so at least I ended my hurling career on a high.

Larry wouldn't have been a great goalie, but he was an amazing man. We shouldn't have been in the Limerick county football championship, for instance. It was like Manchester United entering the Kerry District League. We were too good and they didn't want us either, so they tried every trick in the book to get rid of us. Most of the tricks were used in bureaucracy, because they couldn't beat us on the field.

Not that a few teams didn't try everything they could on the field. We'd be entered in the city championship, and while I loved my college and I loved my football, the only crowd I ever ducked playing against was Treaty Sarsfields in Limerick City. I never played against them for the simple reason that life is too short. I blamed Mick O'Dwyer at the time and told my teammates he didn't want me playing in the game. Treaty Sarsfields are gone now, the club is defunct, but I was in no hurry to meet them when they were still afloat.

Winning the city championship meant you should proceed to the county championship proper, but we knew that winning the city didn't mean we'd definitely be in the county, because we knew the next stage was the objection, one of the great GAA traditions.

On one occasion, it was on the basis of not having Irish watermarked paper for our correspondence, but in all that wrangling, Larry cut his teeth as an administrator and gained valuable experience that stood to him when running for president of the GAA years later.

When we did get out into the county proper, it wasn't always an improvement. In 1976 we played a match against St Kieran's, Carrigkerry, out in Askeaton. The secretary of the Kerry county board, Andy Molyneaux, was from Listowel, near enough to Limerick, and he rang me before that game. He said he'd had lots of phone calls from people who were concerned about my safety if I played against St

Kieran's. It'll tell you what the environment was at that time, because when I drove out to Askeaton for the game – college boys against Carrigkerry – I parked about a mile away from the ground because I didn't feel safe bringing my car any closer.

It was an absolutely filthy match. Carrigkerry had a player sent off, maybe two, but one certainly came back on again and rejoined the game. We beat them. They objected, we counter-objected on the basis of the man being sent off resuming play, which was a pretty good basis for a counter-objection, I thought. But we still lost out to their initial objection: we clearly weren't destined to win that game under any circumstances. The next year we were ready for them, and Larry had dotted every *i* and crossed every *t*.

We won the Limerick championship, we won the Munster championship and we won the All-Ireland. Larry was the man – he drove us. The only regret is that there's no video evidence of the run we had. That's a real pity, because when you talk about great matches a lot of the time that kind of talk is cheap, but if you're talking about great matches in the club championship in particular, the greatest series of matches ever played were the matches between Thomond College and Austin Stacks. This was a four-game series with two of those games going to extra time. There were thousands going to those games in Páirc Uí Chaoimh and the Gaelic Grounds.

We shouldn't have been in the championship, really, but we were in it and we won it. Looking back at my career, two things really stand out – standing on the steps of the Hogan Stand to accept the All-Ireland club championship trophy, and standing on the steps of the Hogan Stand to accept the Sam Maguire. I can't deny it – those are two good ones. A reporter was on to me in 2022 for a piece about great club teams over the years. I pointed out that the Thomond team of 1978 was definitely one of the best ever but it only had one season together because of the nature of college life.

Thomond wasn't just a good team with excellent players, it was also a glimpse of the future of football in terms of preparation. We were doing strength and conditioning, video analysis of games and training, doing walk-throughs of kick-out plays and other moves. Dave Weldrick was an innovative coach who came from a soccer background and imported a lot of those soccer-coaching principles to Gaelic football: give-and-go, pass-and-move, all of those.

We beat St John's of Antrim in the All-Ireland final by fourteen points but there isn't a scrap of video or film of that game, or any other game we played. I'd be confident we'd have handled any county side around at that time with the exception of the top two or three.

The series of games in that championship which is completely forgotten about, of course, is our four games with Austin Stacks in the Munster club championship, which spilled from 1977 into 1978. You can talk about

Dublin and Meath in 1991 but our four games with Stacks in the Munster club semi-final were as great a saga.

In the first game we drew with them in Limerick, 2–6 each, and then we went to Páirc Uí Chaoimh for the replay – another draw, 1–10 to 3–4. We played the third game in Páirc Uí Chaoimh and that ended level after extra time, 2–18 to 3–15: an unbelievable game. We won the fourth game, and don't forget Stacks had won the All-Ireland club championship themselves the year before, with Ger O'Keeffe, John O'Keeffe, Dinny Long, Mikey Sheehy and Ger Power.

* * *

When I left Thomond, I got a gift from my mother. She presented me with a car, a Ford Escort, and that set me up for heading to my first teaching job, above in Listowel.

Almost. I wasn't that well able to drive. While I had a good idea how to go up the gears and go down the gears, I didn't know how to stop the car suddenly, and of course driving through Tralee on my way to Listowel I crashed into another guy on Denny Street. Luckily, he said it was a minor enough job and that a friend of his was a blacksmith and could sort it out. Thank God.

Although I didn't get a lot from the theory, I took a lot from the practice and brought that with me into my first job in Listowel and all throughout my teaching career. I've seen the difference PE makes in a student's life. But on a national level, has PE in schools improved since we left Limerick almost 50 years ago? Not by one iota.

At post-primary level it's still box-ticking, when it comes to senior level most of the time nothing is done at all. At junior level, are they getting the maximum amount of time for PE? Not at all, it's the minimum, and in some cases, it isn't even the minimum and there aren't even facilities. Is it any wonder things haven't improved? Once kids get to Junior Cert, then academics become the priority and PE becomes far less important.

Has PE teaching improved? I would suggest it hasn't. Have youngsters got fitter? No – but I wouldn't blame the PE teachers. That's because you can talk about obesity and fitness and you can have all the investment you want into post-primary schools, but if you don't invest in PE at primary level you can forget about it. That's the problem with obesity, the bad habits, the lack of fitness – it starts at four years of age.

PE in primary schools is non-existent in most cases. There are no facilities and people are not really qualified to teach the subject. There's no inclination to do so, and you'll see it if you drive past nearly any schoolyard in Ireland. Any reader will immediately recognise the scene: two or three teachers having a chat with a cup of tea in their hands and the youngsters are only milling around, most of them on their phones.

When I was teaching in Bantry, what was I getting when the kids came to secondary school? If they were part of a GAA club or another club, fine. The boys, you had them. Unless the girls were part of a club already, when you were encouraging them to get into fitness at 12 or 13, you hadn't a chance.

In sport, no matter what the level or the game, you have to teach kids good habits. Obesity levels are crazy in kids – absolutely out of control – and to remedy that you must have investment in PE in primary schools. You can talk about campaigns to stop kids eating sugar and sweets and fatty foods, but the message has to be about developing good habits rather than cutting out bad habits. Good habits around health and fitness and looking after your body have to be inculcated into the kids from four years of age. If that happens, those habits will carry through.

But unfortunately, it hasn't improved. When I started teaching, I was trying to teach the kids all sorts of activities, like gymnastics. I drew the line at creative dance after studying it in Thomond, though. We used to practice in our own leotards, though thankfully no photographs exist of the 30 of us leaping around imagining we were leaves falling to the ground. In theory it was a great idea and maybe one kid in one hundred might have enjoyed it, but I left that lesson plan in the drawer.

I do remember trying to teach one class how to do handstands until I got a letter from a parent which started

off with: 'If God wanted my son to stand on his head ...'
That kid was excused.

That's teaching for you. It takes all kinds. I learned that
in a place that was like nowhere else in Ireland.

CHAPTER 5

THE KLONDYKE OF SEVENTIES IRELAND

I think it's important to remind people exactly what happened on Whiddy Island.

At around one in the morning on Monday, 8 January 1979, there was a cracking sound heard from the *Betelgeuse* oil tanker as it unloaded fuel at the Whiddy terminal. This was followed by a huge explosion which blew men from the jetty into the sea, and local residents reported seeing the *Betelgeuse* engulfed in a ball of fire minutes later.

On the island, local families had already fled for their lives and 12 hours after the explosion, the *Betelgeuse* sank in 40 metres of water, becoming completely submerged. It was a good fortnight before some bodies could be recovered from the sea. This was a disaster that killed 50 people and changed a part of Ireland for decades, yet it is almost completely forgotten.

The government appointed a tribunal to investigate the incident and it was presided over by Justice Declan Costello. The tribunal took a year to hear evidence and eventually prepared a 480-page report.

* * *

I had just started teaching in Bantry Vocational School. The tribunal of inquiry was out in the West Lodge Hotel, and I felt that it could be as important a part of the kids' education as any geography lesson. It was the first of the real modern tribunals and the start of a slippery slope when you look at the tribunals since. It opened the kids' eyes, and it certainly opened mine.

There were two different stories being given at the tribunal describing the same incident. The locals were giving their version with times and so on which didn't tie in with the version we were getting from other quarters, particularly Gulf Oil, who owned the terminal, and Total SA, who owned the ship.

I thought that was the best education the kids could ever have. The majority of tribunals down the years have been a gravy train for the legal profession, but have never come up with answers, and have certainly not seen justice served for victims.

I look at the Stardust inquiry and I have huge sympathy for those people and for the injustice that they've suffered. But the fact that that happened in Dublin helps it to get more media coverage. Whiddy involved a lot of French people as well as Irish people, but I've always felt it never got the publicity it deserves, which is heartbreaking because it was an out-and-out scandal.

The clean-up wasn't completed until 1983. The cost of salvage was $120 million in all, a huge amount of money at the time, while compensation was paid by Total SA, the ship company, to Gulf.

* * *

That's 44 years ago, and since then it's been a one-man crusade by Michael Kingston. His father, Tim, was one of the people who died at Whiddy. Michael is now one of the top maritime barristers in the world and he's still looking for answers. He's a consultant with the United Nations International Maritime Organisation and a special advisor with the Arctic Council of States. As recently as January 2023 he said he had written to the taoiseach, Leo Varadkar, on behalf of the victims' families seeking a new inquest on the grounds that the original inquest was unreliable, and he had demanded the death certificates to record 'unlawful deaths' and, most importantly, a fulsome apology from the state.

Certainly, I'd be happy if this book could raise the issue and add to their work in any way, shape or form. Because Whiddy has cast a long shadow over Bantry, as we saw in the school for decades afterwards.

Bringing the kids to the tribunal meant they were able to see a scenario unfold before their eyes. They knew what their parents had seen, yet some of the witnesses were flatly contradicting that. So, I was showing them how powerful people can influence matters.

Financially, Bantry did well in some ways from the disaster. I'd estimate there was still work from the clean-up and associated projects going on as late as 1983, so there were four or five good years in it for the town. But then the downturn kicked in. The eighties were a bad time in Ireland anyway, and there was a recession all over the country. That revealed itself in different ways in different places. Bantry managed to get to a county senior football final in 1981, for instance. But most of the players on the team were gone soon afterwards, mainly to America.

Whiddy is important to Bantry's history. It was a difficult time for the town, and we in the school were faced with a lot of difficulties in school as a result. All the social problems meant we were dealing with situations that weren't found anywhere in the country outside inner city Dublin. We had those, if on a smaller scale, in Bantry, which made it very unusual.

There were generations that never worked after the parents or grandparents lost their jobs in Whiddy. Alcohol was a problem and, in latter years, drugs. Huge unemployment led in turn to all sorts of different problems, and we faced a lot of that in the vocational school.

With two schools in Bantry, the secondary school tended to get the high achievers who were heading on to university. The vocational school was considered suitable for all the rest. Some of the town kids came from difficult social backgrounds – and I mean very difficult – but the one thing about them was they were great kids though the deck was stacked against them and they didn't get a fair chance, or a fair start, in life.

I remember one class that was weak enough academically, they weren't interested in school at all. But for geography, my room was a prefab, and we spent six months painting it. We painted the sky on the ceiling and the stars, and we painted the features of a river, we painted different wetlands. It wasn't going to get them past the exam, but I thought they'd know a lot more about geography after that.

Every one of them was a good kid, and there was something good in them. We tried to take the holistic approach to looking after them, but once they went out the school gate to head home in the evening, you couldn't help them, and a lot of them were heading back to tough circumstances.

When the recession hit, it hit hard. Bantry was never the tourist town in West Cork the way Glengarriff was, or

63

Schull, or even Skibbereen. Bantry was just a different town, it was more insular than those.

Bantry vocational school back then was down the Square. Now that building is the courthouse, so when there's a murder in West Cork, I see the accused brought in the doors of the old school.

I was offered a job in St Brendan's College a year after I started in Bantry and I said no. I loved the vocational school until I left in 2011, even though as teachers we picked up a lot of the pieces of the Whiddy aftermath.

There were a lot of single parents in the town, a lot of children born out of wedlock – far more, percentage-wise, than you would expect in a town of that size in the Ireland of that time. Statistics around that time suggested West Cork, with Bantry the main town, had the highest percentage of single parents outside of the Dublin and Cork metropolitan areas.

There were a lot of alternative lifestyles in the town, and we saw that coming through in the schools eventually. And not just in the students. I remember one of the staff who lived on his own in a flat and he drank too much every day, as most of us did. He told me he was chatting one night to a couple of hippies, explaining to them that he found teaching tough, with the struggle to control the class. He said, 'I resort to alcohol to escape and it's costing me a lot of money.'

One of the hippies said, 'Hey, man, we have an alternative that could be a lot cheaper.'

And my friend, who shall remain nameless, said, 'Well?'

'Magic mushrooms,' said the hippie.

He got them and he boiled them, I presume (I wouldn't be an expert on the preparation), and took them. I asked what effect they had.

'I swear to God, Pat, I was still feeling it as I was leaning against the window of the classroom the following day. I looked out the window, and do you know who flew past the window? Cú Chulainn and his hounds. I was still high. I looked at the kids and said to myself, if they only knew what's going through my head at the moment.'

That was Bantry. It was the kind of town where that kind of thing could happen.

* * *

We had a great school, a great principal, good young staff – but we were the 'Tech'. We got the farmer's sons and the lads from the country. The 'good' people from the town, the bright lads and the businesspeople of the town, they sent their kids to the secondary school. When our kids finished the five years with us, did they go to university? Maybe not, but they left better kids and better students than when they came.

At home you knew that some of them were in circumstances in which there was often a dysfunctional family: a drunken mother, drunken father, or no father, maybe kids from several different relationships. I liked to try to get the best out of them and I treated them as … I don't know if 'colleagues' is the right term, but I tried to treat them as friends rather than pupils or students.

It's a different Bantry now, but back then we also tried little things to change it. We organised school tours, which at the time would have been unheard of. Bantry was twinned with a town in Brittany called Pont-l'Abbé so we went to Brittany for a week, immersing them in French culture. We were bringing kids who'd never been beyond Cork to Paris and Brussels. Of course, one time on a night tour of Paris the guy giving the tour was talking about the prostitutes on the side of the street, and the kids didn't know what he was talking about. Innocent times.

We did a tour of Brussels in the early morning, but it was so early that they all slept through it. They woke up because we went to a place called Falkenburg in Germany that had a giant slide, so that was the highlight of the tour.

Would I say I ever really felt part of Bantry? No. I was an outsider who drove in and drove away every day, so becoming part of the community would have been a challenge, but I loved the school and I loved the kids.

What I found very heartening was that, although when I left Bantry I never again went back, a huge number of past pupils sent me cards or messages or text messages when I retired from *The Sunday Game*. It was just unbelievable. People from 20 years, 30 years ago. I'd never been in contact with them since, so I thought that was lovely.

* * *

Eventually we moved premises to a new school, St Goban's, in 1983. Traditionally, the vocational school had the country families supporting it and the weaker town kids, but our vocational school had a lot of things going for it. For instance, we had secretarial classes before the secondary school had them, and of course we were giving them trades, so we were getting them jobs.

When the schools eventually amalgamated, the vocational and the secondary, we'd reversed the proportion of enrolments: there were more going to the vocational than the secondary school. I'd like to think I had something to do with that, but we had other advantages as well. We had a good young staff. I was a PE teacher when not many schools had full-time PE teachers. The change to the CAO system also made a big difference – there were free third-level fees, and better grants, but the big thing was allocating points in practical subjects like metalwork and woodwork. Your A in those subjects also counted in the CAO points race. We also brought in transition year before that became popular.

We had a special needs section in the school, which was one of the first of its kind in Ireland, but it wasn't exclusively special needs – there was a special needs unit in the school but those kids were also integrated into mainstream classes. We would have been ahead of the curve there also.

As PE teacher, I was in charge of all the teams. I'd be taking a bus of 50 fellas – players and supporters – to a match in Coachford or Cloughduv or wherever, then managing the team through the game while also keeping an eye on subs going wild on the sideline – busy times. Training teams was difficult because they were all getting buses home in the evening, so training was at lunchtime – but I loved every bit of it.

* * *

As a PE teacher, are you the best in the world or the worst in the world? Who knows? You can't judge it based on trophies. Geography was different – if they all failed geography, then you knew what your teaching was like. I eventually became vice-principal, and principal, and to be quite honest they were my most satisfactory years.

We never had a hall for PE. The year I retired, they built a new school with a big flashy hall, but for the last seven or eight years before I retired, no hall at all. In the early years we rented a hall down the town, but it was 20 minutes' walk to get to it, which ate up the time for the lesson, so we gave up on that. For the last ten years of my PE teaching my knees were banjaxed, so I stood out in the rain with pain in my legs. I couldn't say I enjoyed that.

Because Bantry had such a cosmopolitan population, we'd be dealing with all sorts of pupils – we'd get home-educated kids who had to come in to do the state exams, and there were very good kids among them. They could be brilliant at English, maths and a language but they wouldn't know where Cork city was. Homeschooling meant they might have no social skills. How did they fare out in college? Disastrously, some of them, and we had loads of them in the school because the hippie or alternative lifestyle was so prevalent there. That meant dealing with a different lifestyle. Different philosophies. I remember asking one mother why her daughter hadn't been in school for weeks. She explained their life philosophy was that the daughter did what she felt like doing. If she felt like dinner in the morning, she had her dinner in the morning, and if she wanted her breakfast at night, she had her breakfast at night. If she felt she shouldn't do homework, she didn't do homework, and if she felt she shouldn't go to school for a couple of weeks, well … In those cases, you were fighting a lifestyle and it was a challenge.

For some reason we also had a lot of Polish kids in the school long before they became plentiful in Ireland. One Polish lad was acting up and we got on to his family. He came in with his dad, who didn't have much English, to meet me and the principal. Our pupil had to translate and we were telling him to tell the father everything that was happening in the school, but the more he said in Polish, the more his father sat there laughing.

I said to the principal, 'This fella is telling the father he's the best student in the school, this is a waste of time.'

* * *

I could see the way education was changing. What was notable was that everyone had a label, everyone was in a category. I saw this in the latter years as a vice-principal and principal; it was all about creating a paper trail. Once the paper trail was created and a report was finalised, everyone involved was happy with their contribution.

There was a case conference one day in Bantry about a young lad in the school whose mother couldn't control him. I was there, his mother, the school psychologist, the garda liaison officer, education welfare officer – eight people, all with their laptops. All ready to produce another paper trail.

The psychologist asked the mother what the boy did when he came home in the evening. She said he liked to break things with his hands. The psychologist said, 'Mr Spillane, it's obvious this boy likes to work with his hands, you've got to change his timetable to allow him to do more practical subjects – woodwork, metalwork and so on.' Box ticked. Problem solved.

The following morning, 11 a.m.: the boy's mother came to the school office to say her car was outside and the boy wouldn't come into the school. I went down with her to plead with him to come into school, the mother crying, and the car was locked.

'Please, come up to school,' I said. 'Your mother's heartbroken.'

'Fuck off,' he said.

Those were his last words in the Irish education system. He's probably still on file somewhere.

Principals and vice-principals are CEOs now. They're administrators. They're not in the corridors, not meeting the staff and the students. They're just behind a computer dishing out reports. People ask if education has changed – of course it has. That holistic approach to developing kids, that's gone. That disappeared 20 years ago because it became all about the points race, rote learning and memorising. The student in the class going to university, were they necessarily the best student in the class? No – but they were able to work within the points race. I look at the way education has been going since Covid and I see a Leaving Cert which has been dumbed down so much that it's become a joke. The points that are being handed out are absolutely unrealistic. It's crazy.

＊ ＊ ＊

We entered the kids in every competitive sport. We were playing competitive sport at ladies' football when ladies' football was unheard of, men's football, basketball, swimming. We brought them to the swimming pool in the West Lodge Hotel to get lessons.

In terms of football, I was in charge of all the teams for almost 30 years, and I put a lot of work into it. In all those years, did Cork GAA ever get in touch to see if I needed footballs, or would I like a coach to come in and help? Like hell they did. From my experience of Bantry, I could say a few things about the GAA in Cork. For one thing, there was no regard for you if you were in charge of the school team because you were 'the Kerry fella, that's Spillane, don't mind him'. Clubs didn't realise or understand the work that was being done, the coaching that was being done to help improve the kids from their clubs.

With school games, getting a pitch in West Cork was like looking for Wembley Stadium: there wasn't a hope in the world of getting one. Soul-destroying. Everywhere they could put an obstacle, they put one in front of the Kerryman.

In my early years as a coach and teacher, I was a lunatic, but I've mellowed completely since. I can remember two schools in particular where there were fellas in charge of teams for their entire teaching careers, and, in honesty, you wouldn't put them in charge of a lunatic asylum. One of them got involved with a Cork team later, which made it even worse.

The system usually worked pretty well. The best referees were public servants who'd rock up to your match in Ballingeary, say, and jump out of the car, ref the match and play no injury time because they were in a rush to Inchigeelagh or somewhere else for another game. Then the clubs had to be paid €20 or €30 to use the pitch for a match, money for the groundsman, supposedly. Of course, most clubs didn't have a groundsman, but if the pitch was anywhere close to a bar, sure enough a drunk would arrive and say he was the groundsman. The local barman had told him there was a handy 20 available from the teachers.

In terms of developing the game and improving teams for Cork, there was no incentive to do that, no joined-up thinking. No idea that there was a bigger picture, potential for improvement if they put in a bit of effort and helped the teacher, no matter where he was from.

Looking across then at Kerry, one obvious question that was often asked was 'Why is Kerry such a successful county?' And one of the answers is the local club is so ingrained with the local primary school and, in particular, with the secondary school. The secondary school in Kenmare is a brilliant example. It produced six players on Kerry's All-Ireland-winning panel in 2022: the four Templenoe lads and the two Kenmare lads. The year before, they had eight on the panel. The success of the school is based on the fact that the kids aren't coached by teachers.

The club lads come in and coach them because they can see it's good for their clubs down the line. The Kerry County Board is good too at putting coaches in the schools and giving resources to the schools.

Sometimes I'd ask about why Cork football, in comparison, wasn't stronger? It may have changed now, but I was in my thirty-third year, my last year teaching in Bantry, when for the first time a coach came from the Cork county board to the school. He took 80 youngsters out to the field in Bantry for an afternoon. What would you get done with 80 kids in one afternoon?

The other factor was the clubs in and around Bantry. Instead of them saying that we were doing a great job, coaching the kids and improving them for the clubs, we were seen as opposition: the Kerry fella.

Once the school was playing a Munster final at U16 against Askeaton in Currow. The night before, the Bantry minors had a West Cork minor league game that was of no importance whatsoever. One of the club mentors rang the Bantry club players that were involved in the school team and told them, 'Your club is more important than the school, forget about Spillane.' A lot of them – not all, but a lot – played in that West Cork league game. Instead of the club having an attitude of helping the school win a Munster title, they took the opposite view. That kind of backward thinking held Cork back for many years. That sense of 'He's from Kerry, so whatever he's for, it can't be in our best interests'. I think that has changed in recent years. I certainly hope it has.

The traditional football areas in Cork are the border areas with Kerry. I know Ambrose O'Donovan, who played alongside me for Kerry, would say that any time Kerry won a Munster final, all the crowd from Gneevenaguilla – his place – and Rathmore would hit for Knocknagree, Bally-desmond and Boherbue in Cork. And vice versa when Cork won, they'd go in the opposite direction.

At a Munster final in Killarney you'd see something similar. If Cork lost, the speed of the Cork cars heading through Kenmare was at record levels: they'd win any rally. If Cork won, though, they spent the night in Killarney or Kenmare, rest assured. If Cork lost, we never got a customer in Templenoe out of the Munster final. If Cork won, it wasn't that they came to drink, but they made the effort to come out and drive past the bar, hooting the horn to celebrate.

Ambrose was always talking about this rivalry, and I could often see it with himself. He was a bit like Lou Ferrigno playing the Incredible Hulk. When Ambrose was lined up in the dressing-room for a Munster final against Cork, he was a different animal: a man possessed. He just had to win. I could see that attitude in Bantry as well – in reverse.

Luckily, I wasn't there for the Munster finals because I'd have been on holidays from school. But take a National

League game – then you'd notice it, and certainly you would notice it around the time of All-Irelands.

I drove that road for 30 years, and I love it. Kenmare, Glengarriff, through the tunnels – it was so scenic that by the time you would arrive into Bantry in the morning, you'd be ready. Mind clear, great form – and the same coming home that evening the other way. For over 30 years, you'd meet the same fellas on the road at the same points – the same council men, the same people getting the paper. For those 30-odd years it was the same for 99 per cent of the time. They went about their business and they ignored you.

But the morning after a Kerry defeat by Cork, or the morning after a Kerry defeat in an All-Ireland final, it was different. They'd flash the car lights. They'd want to stop and chat to you so they could really rub it in.

Sometimes, you'd be thinking, did that hold Cork back? I think it did because it was an obsession. Kerry was the itch. And once Kerry were beaten, they had no other plan – there seemed to be no other rivalry for them.

I went to college with the late Brian Mullins, and he was one of those fellas that if I was picking a team to play with me, he'd be one of them, because he was such a warrior. But if you wanted to annoy Brian, you'd say, 'Brian, you only got your football from your mother's side, the Caseys from Lispole.' He hated everything about Kerry – everything.

I was saying that to a friend of mine after he died, 'Why did Brian hate Kerry so much?'

And the friend said, 'If you were beaten by Kerry in five All-Irelands, you'd hate them as well.' And I suppose he had a point.

It's a bit like that with Cork, particularly the West Cork and Duhallow people. They're like missionaries, brilliant people – absolutely brilliant people – but they're down because their neighbours are winning most of the time. So, there has to be a chip on the shoulder, and I found that in Bantry.

The town has some fantastic natural advantages. They have one of the world's deepest harbours, a beautiful location, and in Rowex they have one of the more successful Irish industries, which isn't really celebrated.

When I retired from teaching in Bantry, I wanted to do something for rural Ireland, for all those places that didn't have those kinds of advantages. But doing that eventually took me to an altogether different place.

CHAPTER 6

LEARNING THE ROPES

The journey began in 1975, and we went into that year's Munster final hungry. Full of belief. Positive. Playing a Munster football final in Killarney was the dream, after all. A hot day, a big crowd, the tar melting on the road, the mountains visible over the stand, the smell of the chips and burgers, the kids with ice cream, the green and gold and red and white, the sun beating down, walking up to the stadium with the crowds before the game, and back down with them to the town to have a pint fifteen minutes after the final whistle …

It was everything. Out of all the games and all the occasions, a good July day for a Munster final was always magic.

＊ ＊ ＊

That day, 13 July 1975, we had huge hunger, but we also had a hell of a lot of luck.

If people remember that game, it's because of the infamous clip of Páidí hitting Dinny Allen a dig about five yards from the referee. Even then, when a lot of games resembled the Wild West, you couldn't do that – it was the most obvious sending-off you could possibly imagine. But all the referee did was get them to shake hands, having slipped on his way over. That was a break for us, because if Páidí had been sent off we could have had no complaints. Winning that game, though, set the tone, and gave us a huge boost in self-confidence.

We played Sligo in the All-Ireland semi-final, and that was another valuable lesson. They'd gotten out of Connacht after decades in the wilderness and had obviously celebrated accordingly. Even then, I'd be looking at the opposition before the game started to see if there were any hints in terms of body language about their attitude, and I saw what I wanted in the pre-match parade.

As the two teams turned in front of the Hogan Stand, the huge Sligo support rose to acclaim the team, and the players across from us were smiling up at them and waving at people they knew. I could tell then that they were just happy to be there, happy to be playing in Croke Park. We were looking at the semi-final as a stepping stone to the final and to an All-Ireland medal, but for them this was the big occasion. We had them, and we beat them handily.

I couldn't have known then, of course, the role Sligo was going to play in my life. I married a Sligo woman, and 47 years after that All-Ireland semi-final, my son Pat lined out for Sligo in Croke Park. Life takes some strange turns, though I can say that the day I saw him run out onto the field in Croke Park wearing a Sligo jersey was one of the proudest moments of my life.

Beating Sligo got us a date with the All-Ireland champions: Dublin.

* * *

The one thing that Mick O'Dwyer looked at with Dublin in 1974 was their fitness, and how Kevin Heffernan had turned them into a machine. He had moved Gaelic football fitness to another level altogether. Their conditioning was far superior to that of any other county.

On the other hand, Dwyer knew he had talent on his side, but the team also had youth and legs – plenty of pace. He said we'd not only match Dublin for fitness, we'd surpass them. If Dublin were the fittest team in Ireland by a country mile, then we'd beat them. And so, the legendary training sessions kicked in.

They were tough, looking back: 30 training sessions on 30 consecutive nights, the wire-to-wire runs, laps of the field. It was savage training at times, but there were a couple of things that helped. Everyone did the training, for one.

There was no shirking. No one crying off with a twinge to have a fag at the side of the field.

More importantly, everyone on the panel was a savage competitor, each driving the other on. I wanted to win all the wire-to-wires, but so did Ger O'Keeffe. So did Ger Power. They all did. No one wanted to be last in any sprint or lap. That's unusual, to have an entire panel who are so driven. There's usually one or two who might be coasting, but not on that panel.

Even the old-fashioned laps of the field were competitive. They might be out of fashion now but they built stamina, and character. The man who was giving it all in February on the fortieth lap, or the tenth wire-to-wire, would give it all in the last five minutes of a Munster final or All-Ireland final.

After those two and a half months of savage physical training, the balls would come out and the sessions became sharp, game-oriented – but no less competitive. Because of all of that, defeat never entered our minds, really. We were rank outsiders, young lads coming up to take on the Dublin machine, but we were confident.

People forget that that game, the beginning of that rivalry, was also the beginning of the saving of the GAA. You had a town-versus-country rivalry, banners on the Hill and in the

Canal End, songs about the teams (most of which were absolutely terrible), the players had long hair and headbands and sideburns, the Kerry side were all bachelors. All of that introduced a soccer-style glamour to the GAA. The scene began to have a bit of sexiness about it. A glamour.

At the start, it was the entire country against Dublin – culchies against jackeens. We had the innocence of youth going into that particular game, and it gave us a freedom; we were under no pressure, Dublin were the favourites. That year also set the template for us for future All-Irelands. That wasn't surprising because Dwyer was superstitious enough – he always wore that green jumper of his, and we sat in the same places on the train up to Dublin, all of those *piseogs*. (What wasn't a *piseog* was Leo Griffin, the kitman, cleaning us all out in poker on those train trips. He was by far the sharpest with cards when there was money on the table.)

What sticks with me about 1975, though, was our arrival in Heuston Station. There were thousands of Kerry people there to line the platform and cheer us through. They'd been on previous trains and gathered to cheer us, and going down past that reception and out on to the bus, you couldn't but be lifted by it. Then it was the routine we'd follow for the next twelve years – out to the Grand Hotel in Malahide, well away from the hype in the city centre.

That evening we'd go for a walk out the beach in Malahide and sit down on the rocks while Micko gave a few words, but it was a chat rather than a big tactical discussion. We never discussed the opposition anyway, but on those Saturday evenings he was really just putting our minds at rest. Sitting there on the beach in the moonlight, you'd look up and see the lights of the planes banking in to land in Dublin Airport and be thinking, 'There's more lads in from London or New York to see us, and they'll see us win it for them tomorrow.'

The next morning: the big fry, the mass, then (for me) the walk to Malahide for two bags of Maltesers. Back to the hotel and sandwiches and tea before heading off to Croke Park, and nobody holding back with the sandwiches either. What was unusual a couple of times in the early years was that Kerry people living out by Malahide would drive us in to Croke Park. The Kerrymen's Association would drive us in using their cars rather than us getting on a team bus, and on at least two occasions we were refused access to a certain gate because we didn't have the right pass or we needed to go to another gate.

We'd have been well aware in 1975 that we were a coming team, with youth on our side. Dublin were at their peak – a lot of them had been playing for Dublin for years already and were nearer 30 than 20, while we had pace and athleticism to burn.

The day of the final was unreal, in retrospect, and for me in particular, because I ended up going to receive the cup. Mickey Ned O'Sullivan was the captain and was carried off injured; he'd won the ball on the halfway line and headed off on a solo run, and he was great to carry the ball. The first Dublin player to come to him was Alan Larkin, who got him in the head with two hands, but Mickey Ned managed to ride that tackle, though it should have been a free. Another Dublin defender got him with a rabbit-punch into the side, another free, while another defender tried to trip him but missed. Mickey Ned then ran into three Dublin players who weren't so much trying to tackle him as hit him head-high, and unfortunately Seán Doherty got him with an elbow. Mickey Ned was carried off and he was never the same footballer after that, though he came back to play for Kerry.

We were so focused that it hardly had an impact on us, and when the final whistle went the head steward, I think, came up and said I'd have to go up for the cup as I was vice-captain (which in itself was news to me).

I've won All-Ireland medals at senior, U21 and club level, and the dream of every player must be to walk up the steps and accept the Sam Maguire, but it was over almost before I realised it was happening. All I remember is that my Irish was no better then than it is now, and I asked someone what 'on behalf of the Kerry team' was in Irish.

I gave the speech and can say with complete confidence it should be listed among the very worst All-Ireland victory speeches ever given. My only defence is that I was 19 years of age and it was my first year playing championship for Kerry. And there I was holding what Páidí used to call the canister.

* * *

The celebrations were bananas, and I mean that. In the Grand Hotel, the victory function, which was always run by the Kerrymen's Association, was held in an indoor riding arena at the back of the hotel. The conditions were just about acceptable for horses, but not ideal for human beings, and certainly not for the numbers that were present for the function, which would have panicked any modern health and safety official.

I was rooming with John Egan and Ger O'Driscoll, and that was an experience in itself. People often asked me what different characters were like in the dressing-room before an All-Ireland final. Páidí would be balls naked, buck-leaping around and shouldering lads, some fellas would be doing their stretches, others would want quiet time just to concentrate, everyone getting revved up – but Egan would be the most laid-back man in the room. Just before we'd go out, Dwyer would be firing us up for battle and Egan might turn to you and say, 'Where are you going for a pint after?' Cool out.

That night in Malahide, we had a kind of suite, with one inside bedroom and then a kind of double bedroom. I was in the inside room but when I got up to the room that night

John had commandeered that room and had invited all of Sneem and Tahilla to stay in the double room. So, the night I won my first All-Ireland I might have gotten an hour or two of sleep, which was doing well given there were about 30 people in the room. So much for VIP treatment for the winners.

Of all the memories of winning All-Irelands, coming down on the train with the cup has to be one of the best. The fog signals going off as you get to Mallow, then on to Banteer, where John Egan's uncle was a garda, the welcome in Millstreet, then Rathmore, Killarney, where you'd go around the streets in a lorry to see the people there to welcome you. Those two or three hours of adulation were what made it all worthwhile. You could never tire of that – more than the medal, maybe, those were the kinds of things that drove us all on.

There's so much talk now about 20-man panels, and the need for plenty of depth – which is right, absolutely – that I look back and shake my head sometimes. Looking at that 1975 campaign, 14 of the players lined out in every game and we only used 19 players, all told. Now, we have impact subs and finishers and so on, but we kept it very tight. Also, while we were known for running up high scores and being an attacking side, we went through 1975 without conceding a single goal, which is fair going.

∗ ∗ ∗

The difference between 1975 and 1976 is simple. In 1975 we were focused, concentrated – and unknown. In 1976, we were heroes, to some extent. We'd come from nowhere and were suddenly being invited to every function under the sun. At one stage there was a suggestion that because we were all bachelors we could serve en masse as escorts at the Rose of Tralee festival that year. Bonkers stuff.

Defending the title in 1976 ... the likes of Mickey Harte, Joe Kernan and Jimmy McGuinness are regarded as being among the greats in management, but one thing they never did was put All-Ireland titles back to back. The problem is a simple one – when you start back training after winning an All-Ireland, you know what's ahead of you. The sacrifices, the effort, and all for what? A medal you already have.

If you're a professional sportsman, the motivation is different – win another title and it's more money. The benefits are obvious. It can be different when it comes to amateurs. You find that you're taking shortcuts you never took the previous year. Instead of 100 per cent, you're giving 99 per cent. You might even miss a session here and there, which was unheard of the year you won. Bits and pieces of that were creeping in during 1976.

The big memory from that year was Páirc Uí Chaoimh, which had been rebuilt. That was a huge development. Now we're used to a stadium being refurbished, but that was a massive undertaking. It was the first modern stadium in the GAA, really, and the first big one built outside of Dublin in decades.

Mind you, if ever a book was to be written about how not to build a stadium it wouldn't have to use a better example than Páirc Uí Chaoimh. It was built in a cul de sac below the level of the River Lee; it looked like something built from plans smuggled out of communist Russia – all grey concrete, no colour. The seats in the stand had no leg room and the dressing-rooms were notorious – the smallest dressing-rooms to be found anywhere in Ireland. A table-tennis team would have struggled to find room there.

The suggestion was that it was built to a soccer stadium blueprint, which might have accounted for the size of the dressing-room, but on the day of a Munster final the subs would be in another room altogether. There wasn't room enough for everyone to be in the one space. Players had to piss in the showers because there weren't enough toilets – the notion that there was room enough to warm up was laughable altogether. You could maybe stretch inside in the showers but you'd have to be careful because another player might be pissing in the shower next to you. To cap it all, you went from the dressing-room to the field via the tunnel under the stand – that meant you were open to spectators while you ran out, people abusing you or giving out an occasional box. Chaotic altogether.

It was typical of the attitude of the GAA at the time that the player was the last person who might have been consulted about the facilities. The spectator was number one, officials were number two and the players came in a long way behind.

My reason for that rant? The shambles that was the 1976 Munster final.

The crowd that turned up in 1976 for the opening ceremony and the final was enormous and spilled out onto the sideline. I often told the story of going in around the Cork goal for a 45 and one spectator, sitting on the endline, hitting me with his umbrella and telling me to fuck off out of it. And I fucked off out the field a bit as well. That was a day health and safety went out the window, certainly, but more than that, there was a powder-keg atmosphere in the place. It wouldn't have taken much at all for the crowd to set off, and the authorities were lucky, really, it was a draw. In one sense it was the ideal result – not just for the Munster Council, but also for everyone's safety.

The replay went to extra time, and we won eventually. John Moloney was the referee, as everyone in Cork remembers. Did we get the rub of the green? Absolutely. We rode our luck. Cork had a goal disallowed that should never have been disallowed, and we got a goal awarded to us which shouldn't have been allowed: Moloney did us a favour that day.

We weren't the finished article at the time. The combinations weren't right and we didn't have players in their optimum positions. But the overall attitude wasn't right either, there's no doubt about that. We had an easy enough win over Derry in the All-Ireland semi-final, which was one of the first times I was accused of throwing myself down and feigning injury. A Derry player, Gabriel Bradley, was holding on to my jersey off the ball, and I was getting sick of it, so I threw myself down on the ground. I make no apologies for doing so. Dwyer covered up me for afterwards, saying I had come in for particular attention. (In fairness, in 1980 when a similar scenario arose with Gerry Fitzmaurice of Roscommon, Michael O'Hehir said I had a reputation for play-acting, and the Kerry county board complained. Years after that, Niall Cahalane of Cork took a similar interest in testing my jersey. He's a gentleman and we're great pals, but I often say to him that if he put all the bits and pieces he yanked out of my jersey together he'd be able to assemble a full one.) It always infuriated me when someone had a hold of my jersey and stopped me from running. You could have Usain Bolt on your team but he wasn't much good if he couldn't move with someone hanging out of his jersey. The linesman was often looking right at the player doing it – the ref himself would glimpse it – and do nothing, so I said, 'Feck this,' and I'd throw myself on the ground.

Then the referee had to stop the game because he couldn't be sure what had happened or if I was hurt or not. They could probably guess I'd thrown myself down but they couldn't be definite, and at least I'd put them on notice, and the referee probably thought, 'I'd better keep an eye on whatever is going on here.'

And it didn't happen as often, once I'd thrown myself down once. I probably shouldn't have done it in the first place but I felt I had no alternative if the officials were turning a blind eye, and I have no regrets about doing so.

* * *

In the All-Ireland final that year, we simply didn't turn up. We weren't good. Why? For one thing, we saw the other side of the innocence of youth. In 1975 we surfed that sensation, no fear and no hang-ups, treating every new experience as it came along. In 1976 we had the innocence of youth in the sense that we thought every year would be like 1975 – that you only had to turn up in September and you'd win an All-Ireland as we had done before.

But Dublin were ready for us. They learned from 1975 what we were like, and from the very first minute they were more physical, more committed, more focused than they had been. There was one advantage in being older as a team – they were physically more mature than us, and mentally more mature as well. We were still a bit giddy after being fêted in Kerry for 12 months, so we were set up for an ambush.

There was also a historic element. That win in 1976 was the first championship win over Kerry since 1934 for Dublin, so there was a bit of motivation there as well.

After the game, I remember reading that there were some in the Kerry county board blaming the loss on a missed training session, though there's more to that than meets the eye. Here's a snapshot of the time: the report stated that Kerry players were complaining of fatigue and wanted a training session cancelled because they wanted to take up an invitation to Beamish and Crawford – and the training session was duly cancelled.

To be fair, Dublin were a great team. The defenders were physically strong, and Brian Mullins was a colossus, literally, in the middle of the field. Tony Hanahoe was years ahead of his time with his off-the-ball running. Jimmy Keaveney was deadly accurate.

What a lot of people didn't realise was that the two teams always got on very well with each other. On the field, we were deadly rivals, but we gelled well together away from games. The teams were similar enough in that both had plenty of intelligent players, high achievers: Paddy Cullen and Seán Doherty were successful publicans, Robbie Kelleher was with Davy Stockbrokers, Tony Hanahoe was a top solicitor, Pat O'Neill was a doctor. They were high-fliers, driven on the field and off the field.

What helped was Listowel – they'd come down there for the races every year and we'd meet up with them and have a great time. They were all good guys – gregarious, good company, outgoing – and when the game was over the game was over, compared to the attitude some other teams had. At Listowel, there were never any recriminations about anything that happened in a game, it was just good fun. And to this day we still have that relationship with them.

* * *

In 2003, my old pal Páidí Ó Sé, who was then Kerry manager, described Kerry supporters as 'the roughest type of fucking animals you could ever deal with'. Páidí was on the money, which is why I don't tend to dwell on GAA histories that discuss 1976 and 1977.

Winning an All-Ireland in 1975 didn't buy us much sympathy with the Kerry public when we lost to Dublin in the next two seasons. Inevitably, when those games are discussed, and others like them, the ones Kerry lost are inevitably classics, while the ones Kerry won are dismissed as predictable, or worse.

After conceding no goals in 1975, we leaked three in the 1976 final. Our defending wasn't at the same level, but in the cold light of day there was one significant difference that meant Dublin were a far better combination in '76 – their half-back line. That year they had Pat O'Neill, Kevin Moran and Tommy Drumm, which was a very modern half-back line compared to previous years – strong, mobile, attacking, aggressive. Three very good individual players who also combined well as a unit.

The 1977 season is remembered now for the All-Ireland semi-final, but our build-up to that game wasn't ideal, because we sailed through Munster. We beat Tipperary by 14 points and Cork by 15 points, which suggested to us we were ready, though we weren't. Cork, for instance, were definitely on the slide compared to the heights of 1973 and 1974. Dublin deserved their win in that All-Ireland semi-final – whatever complaints we might have about 1982 and pushes in the back, they were the better team that day. The scoreboard doesn't lie.

Looking back at the game now, it's clear it was played at a pace that had never been seen up to that point in Gaelic football. The physicality, fitness and work rate were all at a new level, and the ball was pin-balling around the place. It was hugely exciting, and as a sporting contest it would have been hard to find anything as entertaining. The ball was in play almost non-stop, there was no lying down to hold up the play; lads got up straight away if they were fouled, the kick-outs were taken quickly, and frees were just dropped on the ground so the man behind you could run up and blast it straight down the field. It was man on man, each player battling his marker, and the ball was being moved around at a fierce pace. A great spectacle.

Was it the greatest game of all time, though, as people described it? I'd have to say no. The quality wasn't great. Most of the time one team was just booting the ball away to the other team, so the standard of ball retention and accurate distribution was way off. Catch and kick, and not great kicking a lot of the time – the stats boys nowadays would have had a field day taking it apart.

But it was a great contest for its time and of its time. With a lot of modern games, you can close your eyes and you'll know what'll happen – a kick-out means the defending team has retreated, a short restart and the ball is going over and back and over and back … you can nearly go out to boil the kettle for a cuppa because it's all too easy to visualise what's coming in the next two minutes' play. Not that day in 1977, though. Yes, the kicking was atrocious. The number of turnovers was off the scale. Stuff like the drop-kick and first-time pulling on a loose ball were still in vogue.

But it was wildly unpredictable. No one could guess what was going to happen, because it was chaos. If there was ever a sign of a plan on either side, it vanished as soon as the ball was thrown in. Looking back, we were two points up with six minutes to go, and one mistaken sideline decision late on cost us the game.

I can still picture the scene – the ball going loose on the Hogan Stand side of the field and myself and Bobby Doyle, I think, went for it. I went in with a sliding tackle and got the ball – it hit off Bobby and went out over the line, but the linesman gave it to Dublin. (Don't forget, the linesmen that time weren't neutral – they were usually involved with Dublin clubs.) He got the call wrong, Dublin took the sideline, and that led to Dublin's first goal from

David Hickey before Bernard Brogan chipped in with the second. Those are the kinds of small things that can change a game – you're two points up, one decision goes against you and it's a goal.

What nobody remembers is that it was the biggest crowd at an All-Ireland semi-final since 1961 – there were over 55,000 at it – which shows the draw of the two teams. And it was hugely entertaining, as I say. A great spectacle but not the greatest game of all time. People often ask me what was, if the '77 game wasn't, and I always give the same answer. It's subjective, so everyone has their own favourite. But as I said, the great classic Gaelic football games are invariably ones that Kerry lost!

There were positives if you wanted to look for them. We'd been ahead in the closing minutes, so we couldn't be too far off Dublin.

But losing two years in a row to them wasn't good, obviously. Winning in 1975 was all very well but there were doubts about us – team and management – because it looked as though Dublin had figured us out. It's interesting that the next time Dublin beat Kerry in a championship game was 2011, 34 years later, but we weren't to know that in the winter of 1977. We were licking our wounds. Wishing the days away and waiting, waiting, waiting for 1978.

CHAPTER 7

UNBEATABLE

We took those defeats into 1978 as motivation, but the real turning point came 3,000 miles away in New York.

In May 1978 there was a fundraiser for Sr Consilio's Cuan Mhuire addiction treatment centre – a very worthy cause – between Kerry and Dublin in New York's Gaelic Park. The match shouldn't have been played at all because the pitch was waterlogged but, lucky for us, it went ahead, because that game was the reason we went on to win so many All-Irelands afterwards.

We laid down a marker that day in New York. Dwyer had been saying we needed to do that after being beaten by Dublin in a few games, because that belief was beginning to trickle into our own thinking: maybe they *are* better than us. We discussed it – one of the only times we considered the opposition – and we asked ourselves what the difference was between the two teams? What separated us?

We felt the difference was in physicality. When we fouled them it was a push in the back or a tug of a jersey, a harmless misdemeanour; the game rolled on and it took nothing out of them. We found that when they fouled us, they hit us – they got value for the free that was given away because they were belting us, and that eventually wears a player down, that punishment. So, that May morning, we made a conscious decision that we weren't going to lay down. If they hit us, we'd answer. We'd meet fire with fire and be just as physical.

As a result, it was the filthiest game I ever played in.

There were three players put off and there could have been another nine given the road. I broke my nose – or had it broken – and Jimmy Deenihan got a similar dose. One of the Dublin backroom team happened to come through after I got injured, but he refused to reset my nose, so I had to get the on-site doctor to look at it. Clearly, as part of a box-ticking exercise, John 'Kerry' O'Donnell, who ran Gaelic Park for years, had to have a doctor present for games, and I found him somewhere in the ground, an old Italian chap holed up in a small room reading the *New York Times*.

He looked up over the paper and said, 'What's wrong?'

'I think I've broken my nose.'

Without putting the paper down, he told me to head over to the mirror on the wall.

'Tell me this,' he said. 'Does it look different to how it looked this morning?'

'It does, it's sideways across my face.'

'Well, you've probably broken your nose. There's not much you can do about it.'

And that was that.

But we certainly laid down a marker. We believed, leaving Gaelic Park, that we had gained the upper hand, and we beat them from 1978 to 1986. We won seven All-Irelands and beat Dublin in four of those finals. After the New York game in May 1978, Dwyer gave a typical comment: there was no deliberate policy to get involved, he said, but added that we weren't going to be pushed around, that we wouldn't stand for that. So, work out what he meant by that!

* * *

How did the year pan out? We played Waterford in the first round and won by 25 points, we beat Cork by 7 points, beat Roscommon by 12 points, and in the final we beat Dublin by 17 points. We scored 15–63, an average of 0–19 a game, and we conceded 5–32, an average of just over 0–9; our average winning margin was 0–15. We were purring.

The team was beginning to click into shape. Jack O'Shea and Seán Walsh were settling into the midfield partnership we needed, and another missing part of the jigsaw slotted in up front – Eoin Liston, the Bomber. He was a huge asset because he quickly became our Plan A and our Plan B. He was a target man, a ball-winner with great lateral vision and quick hands. He knitted it all together.

Sr Consilio. Midfield partnership. Bomber. Those were signs it was all coming together for us. And time was beginning to catch up with Dublin, too. We weren't even at our physical peak yet, while they were in decline by 1978.

Not that you'd have thought that 20 minutes into the All-Ireland final. We were on the ropes, frankly. Dublin started in a whirlwind and dominated us totally. I didn't touch the ball in the first 16 minutes, an entire quarter of the game, even though I was roving all over the field. That was in keeping with expectations – most pundits had picked Dublin, no doubt based on how they'd handled us in the previous two years. Not for the first time, it was John Egan who got a goal to settle us down. And then we got the softest, handiest free of all time for Mikey Sheehy's famous goal.

Was a free committed by Paddy Cullen? Not at all, but Mikey still had to curl it into the net from a tight enough angle. Michael O'Hehir described it on commentary as the greatest fluke of all time, but it wasn't. It was one of the greatest strokes of genius of all time – only Mikey Sheehy would have thought of trying for a goal from that free.

To think about it was one thing, but executing it, with no run-up, Paddy Cullen running back, on the wrong side for a right-legger, in an All-Ireland final? Of all the players in Ireland to be handed the ball in those circumstances, he was the right man. Don't forget that he was offered a trial with Southampton as a youngster. He always had a beautiful touch, great skills. When you talk about people like Colm Cooper, Maurice Fitzgerald and David Clifford, Mikey is very much in that category. He could make the ball talk, which is a meaningless cliché until you see a player like him in action. That clip should be shown on coaching courses as it illustrates how a player can go off-script when it counts, that it doesn't have to be safety first all the time. Con Houlihan's famous phrase about Paddy running back like a woman who's realised she left the cakes in the oven was completely accurate, but for me, I always remember the look on Paddy's face when his arms were around the post after the ball landed in the net. The game was over after that, really.

It was a curious final for me. The *Evening Echo* in Cork did a statistical analysis of the game a couple of days after and found that I didn't touch the ball for the first 16.5 minutes of play. Then I made 32 plays for the rest of the game, which meant I was on the ball every 45 seconds, on average, including the couple of minutes I spent as goalkeeper towards the end.

It all worked out well. I ended up with the Footballer of the Year award for that year. There was another twist to that season for me in that I won an All-Ireland club title with Thomond College, which put the icing on the cake.

* * *

The following season, 1979, that Kerry team was at its absolute best. I genuinely think we were unbeatable that year. The team was settled. Everyone was fit and at or near their physical peak. The formula was right, everyone knew their job, and we were really rolling. One of the lads who liked a punt made an absolute fortune by backing us to win comfortably in games, and he was right, because I couldn't see any team beating us.

I think the other factor was fear, though. We were driven by memories of 1976 and 1977, and specifically a fear of being beaten because we weren't ready or we hadn't prepared properly. We were sure we'd be ready, mentally and physically, no matter what the challenge was. In winning the All-Ireland, we used three substitutes that year. That's why, when people talk about the greatest team of all time, I mention that team and that year.

It began with us beating Clare in the famous 'Milltown massacre'. A lot of people might remember that we beat them by 36 points, but few remember that Clare's score against us that day, 1–9, was the highest we conceded for the entire championship. We beat Cork by 10 points, beat

Monaghan by 22 points, beat Dublin by 14 in the final. We averaged 30 points a game and a concession of 10, so our winning average was around 20 points a game.

The great Dublin team of recent years used more players than us, but our winning margins in the big games were far bigger – they were demolition jobs. We had the right age profile, the right management, the right blend of players and all of them fit – and other teams were getting demoralised because they weren't reaching our fitness levels. For us, it became a virtuous circle.

In other years, it wasn't as straightforward. In 1980, we were missing Bomber for the final, a huge loss. I was injured for 1981 and for 1982, and Jimmy Deenihan was out injured for '82 as well, another huge loss.

So, the 15 players in 1979 provided the perfect blend. A question people sometimes asked was whether anyone was pushing hard to get into the team, or whether there was anyone who got a raw deal in Kerry, maybe a good club player who didn't get a fair chance to make the county team in that period? At the time, we played along. I got 3–3 in the Milltown massacre, and I remember saying in an interview afterwards that we kept the foot down in that game because we were mindful that we could be replaced easily enough, but that wasn't the case. Dwyer had the best 15 on the field by far, which probably came against him later in his career – because the unit was so tight it probably militated against trying newer lads and testing them out for inter-county football. Before we even played in 1979, though, I had a distraction.

* * *

If you Google 'Superstars Ireland' or 'Superstars competition Ireland', one of the first images you'll be treated to is the Pat Spillane tan. Eye-catching though that was, there was a lot more to *Superstars*, which was a TV show that pitted sportspeople from various fields against each other in a variety of sports and skills.

ABC, one of the American TV channels, devised the show and, for a while, it was hugely successful. It wound down when it transpired that highly paid professional athletes didn't appreciate being beaten by unknowns and amateurs, but what really banjaxed it in Ireland was lads with no real profile specialising in the particular disciplines to win them.

I'd never seen it, but I competed in the competition in Newpark School for the Irish version. David O'Leary was with Arsenal at that time and he was very good, but he had to go back to Arsenal and didn't complete the events. Pat McQuaid the cyclist, Mick Dowling the boxer, Pat Hartigan the hurler – those were the kinds of athletes involved.

I won in 1979. Bernard Brogan of Dublin won it the following year, but then lads from sports like canoeing started to win it, athletes who didn't have a huge profile, and it started to lose its appeal.

But going back to March 1979, a couple of days after winning the Irish version I was on a plane to the Bahamas to take part in the international version. In fairness, they put us up in the Grand Bahama in Freeport, the lap of luxury – I had a personal servant for the week who collected my gear and carried my belongings around.

Because it was March, there were no games I was missing, but I wasn't in top condition either. I'd have been reasonably fit without being in championship shape. That was a slight drawback (not an excuse, just an observation) but what was a significant drawback was the heat in the Bahamas, which was really oppressive. I was also against professional athletes. Some of them were retired but they were in good shape – they certainly hadn't let themselves go. You'd recognise the difference in these lads as professionals. Physically they were very impressive; even if they were retired, they'd lived and behaved as professionals for years and that had to have an effect. They were also painstakingly meticulous in their preparation. They had personal trainers and they'd trained specifically for individual events.

Brian Budd was the reigning champion, and he won that year as well; he was a Canadian soccer player for the Vancouver Whitecaps, and a great guy. He was a good friend of Ray Treacy, who'd played for Vancouver along with Johnny Giles.

Budd came to Ireland for a holiday, but the weekend he picked to arrive coincided with the Pope's visit. Ray rang me and said to come up to Dublin, I could stay with him and we'd meet up with Brian for a few drinks the night before the Pope's mass in the Phoenix Park. As a mark of respect for the Pope, though, the pubs of Dublin closed at teatime the night before the mass, and the only establishments open were the wine bars along Leeson Street. I'm a pint drinker, not a wine drinker, so that night with the lads I had pints of wine and orange juice. Some brainwave: I got violently sick and never had a worse hangover, and I've never drunk wine since. When I woke up in Ray's house I struggled out of the bed and went downstairs.

'I better get going to that mass, Ray,' I said.

'Come in here,' he said. 'There's about five minutes of it left on television.'

In the Bahamas, Budd was by far the best at the competitions, and he came first: he won $38,800 dollars, which was a tidy sum. Peter Snell, the great New Zealand runner, Dwight Stones, the high jumper, and Jim Taylor, an American footballer, also figured.

What did I learn from the experience? I picked up a lot about the psyche of the American sports star and how important psychology was. For instance, I remember chatting to Jim Taylor before the 800 metres event and he nonchalantly said, 'Ah, if I don't do this first lap in 58 seconds I'm not going to be in contention, but I'm expecting 58.' In my mind I was thinking, 'Hang on, 58 seconds is around the Irish national record,' so he had that doubt put in my mind.

And a little like the Ulster teams facing Kerry, once I realised that I was as fast as Taylor it was far too late – he was gone and I was playing catch-up. So, the importance of getting an advantage over an opponent like that wasn't lost on me, whether it was by a suggestion or a comment or something before an event.

The other lesson maybe related to American sport in general. There was a tent full of pharmaceutical products on site, medications to help you with a cold, or hay fever, or bandages for strapping. But there were plenty of other products there as well, and I have no doubt lads were getting injections for other reasons too.

The format was interesting. If you won the event you got ten points, second seven points and so on. Ten points equalled $3,000 roughly, so one point equalled about $350. We were choosing our events, and because I was last to choose I noticed only four had picked the 400-metre swim, which meant that, even if I came last, I'd still get $350. I wouldn't be a great swimmer, I'd be slow, but I entered the swimming and came last – by a large margin. But I still got my $350.

The half-mile bike race, I came fourth, and I clocked 10.64 in the 100 yards, which was good going. Greg Pruitt, a Hall of Fame running back with the Cleveland Browns, won: he was the speedster.

The one event I thought I had a chance with was soccer. You started 20 metres from the goal, dribbled around two cones and had a shot. The goalkeeper was American – and terrible – so I felt confident that I had the ball skills to do well. I had the $3,000 in my pocket before I even started. But I made an amateur error. Instead of focusing on making sure I scored, I tried to do it too fast and was going 100 miles an hour, and I ended up missing the chances. Instead of making $3,000, I made nothing, and I was disgusted. Even worse, I refused to do a TV interview afterwards because I was so disappointed – and it was Jackie Stewart, the racing driver, conducting the interviews. I was even more disappointed when I realised later who it was.

The one bright side was that the American TV company felt it might be entertaining to have a kicking competition between myself and Rafael Septien, a placekicker in the American National Football League, because they found out that Gaelic football was a kicking game. I'd never taken frees in Gaelic football, but I said I'd compete anyway. We took five kicks each, from 20 metres, 30 metres, 40 metres, and he only beat me on the fifth and last kick.

I know Tommy Furlong of Offaly did well in American football, but what I found was, coming from Gaelic football, it was hard to get the ball into the air quickly over the players rushing out to block you.

Then they asked me to punt the ball, to put it high and long, and I was able to boot it a mile. Someone in the crowd was attached to the San Diego Chargers and I was invited to a tryout there in the Bahamas. The Chargers' man was impressed and invited me to another tryout with the team in San Diego. We had an All-Stars tour in Los Angeles at around that time, and I was tempted. It would have been the easiest gig in the parish, but we had won the All-Ireland and I knew there were good times ahead. The Chargers said they'd look after me for the few days, but I said no. At times you'd wonder how it might have gone, but I know well that if I'd made it with them at this stage, I'd probably be on my fourth divorce and my third stint in rehab. Maybe it was just as well.

I never met any of them again – apart from Budd on his Pope's visit – but it was an amazing experience. I'd have liked to go to it when I was at peak fitness – that was my only regret. As it was, I came home with $2,100 in my back pocket. Jimmy Magee was covering the event for RTÉ, and I can remember asking him to play down the prize money element in case the Revenue took an interest, but the memories were worth a lot more.

★ ★ ★

The following year, 1980, was all about the three-in-a-row, and because we'd been so dominant the year before, steamrolling teams, we got a bye through to the Munster final. Talk about a vote of confidence. We played three matches, then, to win an All-Ireland that year. These days it's seven matches and you mightn't even be in the final.

We were in cruise control against Cork, winning by ten points, but there was a classic semi-final against Offaly. That game probably gave Offaly a sense that they were on the right track. It was the day Matt Connor hit 2–9 in what was one of the finest individual displays I've ever seen. When you talk about great players, he was one of the classiest of the class acts. Stylish, two-footed, great balance, great temperament, just a brilliant player. My brother Mike was on Matt and saw how good he was up close.

The game itself was the definition of an old-fashioned shoot-out, 4–15 to 4–10. It wasn't that we took Offaly lightly or underestimated them – to be honest no other team was on our radar at that stage. We expected to win every game and it worked out like that more often than not; we cruised past most teams. We certainly expected to cruise past Roscommon in the All-Ireland final.

That game ended 1–9 to 1–6, one of the lowest-scoring totals in an All-Ireland final ever. It was certainly the worst All-Ireland final I ever played in, our worst victory in an All-Ireland final, and I'd say it was probably one of the worst All-Ireland football finals ever played. It was a terrible game. We were bad on the day, certainly. One of the reasons for that was Bomber didn't play – he had to cry off late in the week to get his appendix out. That removed our target man and upset the balance of the team.

We didn't realise it at the time because we were so focused on the job at hand, but it was a major issue because when all else failed out on the field that option was always our fall-back: lump it in high to Bomber on the edge of the square. The slick passing was usually enough but if you were caught or bottled up, you could drop the ball in on top of him and he'd either win it or break it down to one of the other forwards. That lifeline was gone, and late enough in the day. He'd been part of our plans all along, and finding out he was gone a couple of days before the game didn't give us much time to consider an alternative, let alone practise one.

We were also bad on the day, quite apart from that, and Roscommon were well and truly up for the game. They went through and got a goal after just 35 seconds, which told you everything about their attitude.

They had us on the rack, absolutely, but they also had a particular plan, to stop us playing by fair or foul means, whether on or off the ball. They were on top, and we were struggling, but they became defensive. Winning easily enough with Kerry on the ropes wasn't part of their plan at all, and they became far too defensive.

There were 64 frees in the game and we got 41, which tells its own story, not to mention the 6 bookings. A long time afterwards, someone who'd been in the Roscommon dressing-room told me he'd been very disappointed in their team talk before the game, because it was more along the lines of a speech to give soldiers heading out to war than footballers going out to play a game.

There's no point in sugar-coating it: they left an All-Ireland title behind them because they were too negative, too cynical and too defensive. We got out of jail completely the same day. There's no point in sugar-coating that either.

* * *

Was it a sign that we'd gone past that 1979 peak? Maybe. We were still seen as unbeatable and we were still better than what was around, but we weren't quite at that level we'd reached, even though that sounds like nitpicking.

I think Dwyer noted that we'd lost a little bit of an edge around 1980. It's no coincidence that the carrot of the round-the-world trip was introduced in 1981. The five-week holiday was motivation. Certainly, the four-in-a-row and immortality and all of that were motivating factors, but the prospect of that holiday was driving us all the time.

Our first-round game against Clare that year was played in Listowel, not even a county ground. That showed that our dominance was having an impact that wasn't altogether positive when you could play a Munster senior football championship game in a club ground. Later in the year, the All-Ireland football final drew 10,000 people fewer than the hurling final. It meant nothing to us at the time. Our focus was on each game as it came – we beat

Clare that day by over 20 points – and in the Munster final the scoreline was 1–11 to 0–3. Cork got one score from play in the entire game.

What's worth pointing out, though, is that the first half of that Munster final was the real birthplace of the blanket defence in Gaelic football – not the Northern coaches borrowing Clive Woodward's ideas, or Joe Kernan's double sweeper, not Mickey Harte's swarm defence, not Jimmy McGuinness and his Taliban-type defence.

The first half of that Munster football final featured all of the innovations mentioned above because it was only when the ball was thrown in that we realised the strength of the breeze that day. It was a gale-force wind that was backing Cork in the first half as they played into the dressing-room end.

We realised fairly quickly we weren't going to score too much into that wind, and unconsciously we retreated en masse back the field to stop Cork getting a shot at goal. In the second half, we had the wind so we opened up and blitzed them.

So, it may come as a shock to our Northern brethren to hear that admission from the man blamed all over Ulster for condemning that negativity – that the blanket defence was born in Killarney in 1981. It was pure pragmatism. Needs must.

We beat Mayo easily in the All-Ireland semi-final – 16 points the final margin – but that was when I hurt my knee in a nondescript club game, one that every participant had probably forgotten within 24 hours. Except me. It was a turning point in my career, I just didn't know it at the time.

CHAPTER 8

RATS AND REHABILITATION

It was a run-of-the-mill club league game for Templenoe against Waterville over in Fr Breen Park in Kenmare and an innocuous passage of play. It was August 1981 and I was absolutely at my peak, 25 years of age, when I tore my cruciate.

I felt it snap, there was no doubt about it, and it came about because of a little trick I'd been using for a couple of years by then. When I got the ball, I liked to let the defender come right in close to me, then I'd dig my left heel into the ground and pivot, which worked particularly well in wintertime. I'd stop suddenly, pivot, turn and go the other way, but obviously that was putting my leg under huge strain – the manoeuvre was forcing my ankle to stay in place while my knee was bending to spin away. Eventually, that force tore the ligament.

Up to then, I'd never been injured, never pulled a hamstring or anything like that, but I knew I was in trouble immediately. It was a beautiful summer evening, but more importantly it was also the night of the Munster Fleadh Ceoil, which was on back in Kilgarvan. And of course, I went to the Gala Ballroom for the Fleadh that evening, though my knee was in bits. Agony.

I'm not a dancer usually, but there was plenty of drink involved that evening, so I went out for the 'Siege of Ennis' and the 'Walls of Limerick' and plenty more besides. The following morning, I paid for it. The pain was one thing but the knee swelled up like a balloon – which you might think of as a figure of speech, but which was absolutely accurate in this case. It was huge.

I was still at home and my mother needed help in the bar at the height of the summer, so down I went behind the counter for the rest of the day, which was no great help. Eventually the pain subsided to a certain extent, and later, when I got it seen to, there were other complications. Because my leg muscles were so strong at that stage, many of the tests that were used to measure instability in the knee didn't show anything, so the medics felt I might be alright.

The knee was unstable, it was still sore, and I had a nagging sense there was something wrong. But the four-in-a-row was also looming: the All-Ireland final against Offaly was on the horizon and I obviously wanted to be involved.

I trained away with Kerry but I was cute. The straight-line running was no problem, but I made sure to skip anything which involved twisting and turning, while I also minded myself through the backs and forwards sessions. By that, I mean I minded myself by keeping well away from Páidí in those sessions.

In fairness, I told Dwyer I was hurt. I wasn't dishonest, and he minded me, but he still had to make his mind up about starting me in the final. The night before the game, he and Dr Dave Geaney, the Kerry team doctor, brought me to St Brigid's ground in Blanchardstown. They put me through a fitness test, and I passed it, but even then I knew I wasn't ready. To the naked eye, I might have looked ready but I knew I wasn't, and I told them I couldn't play in the final.

I've often had people say to me that I was selfish as a footballer, and that's always been my retort: if I was truly selfish, I'd have started that All-Ireland, but it wouldn't have been fair to the rest of the team.

Over the years, I have forgotten a lot about the games I played in. Some details stay with me while other passages I can't recall at all. But one thing I've never forgotten is the feeling of sitting in the dugout in Croke Park before that game started, and the other players refusing to let the photograph be taken until I came out for the picture.

I can think of plenty of enjoyable memories, but that's one of the greatest, and it had nothing to do with kicking a ball or getting a score. They were recognising what it meant to me to miss out on a game and calling me out for the photograph was a huge thing for me. So was getting on the field for the last few minutes. Dwyer put me on late in the game at a time when there were only three subs allowed, and he didn't tend to make too many changes during a game. So, I won the medal on the field of play. That was magic.

Looking back now, winning four in a row was a doomsday scenario of sorts for me. It meant the five-in-a-row was on the horizon, so I wasn't about to jeopardise my involvement through a serious operation to repair the knee.

Owen McCrohan was our masseur and physio, and through contacts in the North he was able to access various machinery and equipment. He got electronic pads for my knee, and Owen liked to show people that I could take the maximum electrical charge in my knee. It didn't bother me, but my leg would be hopping up and down with the electric charge. At the time we thought we were doing great stuff with the leg, but in reality, we were probably doing more harm than good. I had Amy Johnson helping me in Dublin, but Clare Edwards kept me going in Kerry by putting me through physiotherapy sessions in Killarney that kept me on track with the team.

From September 1981, my focus was on being involved in the five-in-a-row, but I wasn't ready. We decided the best course of action was to build up the muscles even more around the leg – the quads, the hamstring, the calves – in order to compensate for any weakness in the knee. And I did.

That meant savage work. I had a weights machine in the garage of the house, and it was like an extension of my body for that year, and for another nine years after that to maintain the strength in my legs. Every second day, almost all-year-round, I worked that machine. It was cold in the garage some nights, very cold, but I'd still go out.

That was where the drink for the bar was stored, so you'd hear the scuttle some nights and know there were rats running around. I might be doing a hamstring curl, lying flat on my stomach, and from the noise, I'd know there'd be a rat perched up behind me … but I kept going. Was there ever a day I missed? No. If it was Christmas Day or New Year's Eve and I had a session scheduled, I went out and did it, rats or not.

I got there. At half-time in the All-Ireland final of 1982, I came on – but I wasn't right. My knee was weak and I knew it wasn't 100 per cent. I was operating at 50 per cent at best and couldn't go into 50-50 challenges with any confidence. Should I have played? It was Kerry's biggest game ever, a chance at five in a row, and I felt I could contribute, and I did score a point. I wasn't a liability, but I wasn't fully fit. If I had been 100 per cent I'd have been a better asset for Kerry, and certainly if Jimmy Deenihan had been fit to play that day I think we would have won, but that's water under the bridge.

In 1982 the writing was probably on the wall in Páirc Uí Chaoimh in the Munster final when we drew 0–9 apiece with Cork. That wasn't a good sign. Yes, we won the replay well, and we went on to beat Armagh in the All-Ireland semi-final, but there were other worrying signs for the final itself.

I was still injured but more importantly, probably, was that Jimmy Deenihan was out. He'd broken his leg that summer, and as the main man-marker he was a huge loss because the area in front of our goal was his province. As it turned out, that was exactly the area where the game was won and lost.

Experienced as we were, the hype around the five-in-a-row was notable. The T-shirts. The song by Galleon. The non-stop talk about it. Sometimes the media flipped that back on us a little, suggesting we were arrogant, but that genuinely had nothing to do with us. We were hardly going to be singing a song about winning five in a row ourselves; we'd been on the road since 1975 and weren't about to give away any hostages to fortune like that.

Did it affect us, though? Yes. It got to us. We had more experience than almost any other team in history at that stage, but the pressure still got through to us, and it got through to us with about 20 minutes to go in the game itself. Suddenly, the realisation came through that we were on the brink of something huge. I only looked at the game again recently, which is something I'd never done before. I often told people who asked me about it that it'd be like looking at a video of your own funeral.

I couldn't get over it. With the last quarter upon us, it was clear that our mindset was: 'What we have, we hold.' You had Mikey Sheehy going back into defence, Jacko dropping back to mind the square, kicking the ball out the field to where he should have been himself.

We sat back to protect our lead but that meant kicking the ball back out, handing possession back to Offaly and enabling them to come at us in waves. And eventually we cracked. We missed a penalty. If we'd scored that, would we have won? Possibly. I know Mikey has said since that there was no great rush of fellas to take the ball off him so they could hit the penalty, and that's a fair point: there wasn't.

I came on as a sub and got a point with my first touch from play, which was great, but while I was fit, I wasn't match-ready. If I'd gotten a belt into the side of the knee it was gone, so I had to be very careful. I didn't make a mess of things when I came on, but I certainly didn't play the way or at the level I'd reached in other finals.

We lost, and I have no arguments. We lost by a point and we're not into recriminations and begrudgery in Kerry. But the referee, PJ McGrath, did what a lot of weak referees do late on in that game – he gave handy frees to the losing team. I'll make that case until the day I die.

We were four points up and cruising and he gave two frees against us that I'll argue with anyone, having watched them on video over and over again, but Offaly scored both. One was given against me. I was going down to pick up the ball and Johnny Guinan ankle-tapped me as I did so. I fell down on top of the ball, but instead of getting a free, the referee gave a free against me. Presumably, it was for touching the ball on the ground, but the only reason I did so was because an Offaly player had tripped me. Should never have been a free.

The second example was even worse. Seán Lowry was in possession of the ball and was surrounded by three Kerry players. Not a tackle in sight, our lads knew well the ref was only looking for an opportunity, but Seán threw himself forward with the ball and won a free. No contact, but a second soft free.

The goal that Offaly's Séamus Darby got … you can say it was a nudge or a slight push or whatever way you want to describe it, but it was a foul, pure and simple. That was 1–2, game over. We lost our chance at history and Offaly won an All-Ireland. Do I begrudge them? Not a bit, but those are the facts. It's not opinion, but facts: they got 1–2 that shouldn't have been awarded.

In the dressing-room afterwards, everyone was crying. Without exception. Something I didn't tell people for years after was that I went into a cubicle myself and cried for two or three minutes, maybe more. But when I came out, that was it. Maybe I came out a different person, but I came out of that cubicle saying to myself, 'Feck it, I'll get the knee operated on, this isn't going to be my final appearance here in Croke Park.'

The only fella I can remember being relaxed about the whole thing in the dressing-room was John Egan. He was the one saying, 'Okay, lads, it's only a game, come on.' He was the one being calm, as the captain, but I think it affected him more than anyone else. I believe he bottled up the effect of that loss more than anyone else; he never showed the kind of emotion we might have expected. As the captain, he was to have Sam Maguire in his own club, Sneem, when we won, and that was due to be the biggest night ever in the history of Sneem. The pubs had ordered in dozens of extra kegs, thousands of people were going to descend on the village for the celebration.

I remember the actual night we went to Sneem, with no cup, and standing on the back of a lorry outside Dan Murphy's bar, on a miserable evening. We had great nights over the years, obviously, parading around Killarney and Tralee with Sam, but if you wanted the opposite experience, then standing on the back of a lorry in front of a couple of hundred people on a wet Tuesday evening in Sneem is a good example. That's the difference between success and failure.

The only good side is that, had we beaten Offaly, I believe most of the team would have packed it in then and there. What else would there have been to win after five in a row? I think a lot of the players thought to themselves:

'This isn't going to be this team's epitaph.' I think instead of losing one All-Ireland in 1982, we went on to win three more between 1984 and 1986.

* * *

It was terrible to lose, obviously, but if we'd won that day I think it would have been over for a lot of us. I certainly would have been thinking, 'I'm 26, 27, I've won everything, do I really want to keep going?' That said, I was a fanatic, so I probably would have kept at it anyway, but losing made my mind up. I was hell-bent on getting back to my best because I wanted to leave on my own terms rather than being forced out by injury.

I was involved with Bantry that year in the Cork championship – they got to the county final but were beaten by Nemo, and we had an almighty piss-up the night of the final. The next evening, I checked into the Regional Hospital in Cork for an arthroscopy at around 11 p.m. God be with the days you could do that. The following morning, I was in the corridor at 7 a.m., ready for action, and badly hungover, when the machine was rolled in. Unfortunately, it had round plugs and the socket only suited square plugs, so the electrician had to be called but he didn't get in until 9 a.m. It's no fun hanging around for a few hours like that if you're stone-cold sober, but I certainly wouldn't recommend it while you're suffering a hangover.

Eventually, the arthroscopy was done, and the orthopaedic surgeon visited me that evening with the great Dr Con Murphy.

'Well, what's the story?' I asked.

'You've ruptured your anterior cruciate ligament,' said the surgeon.

'Is that serious?'

'Very serious.'

'Will I play football again?'

'No,' he said. 'Never.'

And the two of them left.

In fairness to Dr Con, he has been a great friend to me all my life. If I could, I'd write a book outlining everything he has done for me, and all my teammates, and it wouldn't be a short volume either. I can't praise him enough. He came back to the room a few minutes later and sat down by the bed. He knew it was the end of the world for me, hearing that verdict at the age of 26.

'Look,' said Con, 'there's a chance.'

He was probably just trying to give me a lift, but by saying that he encouraged me hugely. We all know what the anterior cruciate ligament is now. So many famous sportspeople have ruptured theirs over the years, but we were dealing with the unknown back then, so I started doing my research.

* * *

The knee's a badly designed device at the best of times, but the anterior cruciate ligament (ACL) stops the bone from sliding forward, and when it ruptures it's a very serious problem for the knee. Once I started researching, I found that there didn't seem to be a single sportsperson in Ireland who had ever resumed sport after that injury.

What I also learned, though, was that at that stage, 40 years ago, geriatric surgeons were used to dealing with elderly people who often presented with broken bones rather than sportspeople. They couldn't understand the motivation of someone who had done so much damage to his leg on a football field, yet wanted to get back to that football field and probably do even more damage to his leg. Sports medicine was non-existent in Ireland, really. I resorted to all sorts of cures – people all over Ireland sent me holy water, poultices, everything – but I was trying to find someone who could offer me hope for the future.

My uncle, Canon Michael Lyne, parish priest in St Michael's, Glasgow, was also the unofficial chaplain to Glasgow Celtic. Every Monday he'd play golf with Jock Stein, Seán Fallon and Dr John Fitzsimons, the team doctor. He made inquiries, and through those connections, David Hay, who'd played for Celtic, found out that someone had come through the cruciate injury. George Burley of Ipswich Town, who managed Scotland years later, had returned to play the game at the top level. The man who operated on Burley was David Dandy of

Cambridge. Dandy had returned from Colorado, where he'd had plenty of practice on knees because there were so many skiing injuries in that area.

Through Con, we made contact with Dandy, and he operated on me in October 1982. The Kerry county board paid for some of it, the VHI paid for some, but I paid for a lot of it because I was so focused, so determined to get back playing.

After the operation, I picked up a serious infection in hospital and was kept in intensive care for a good 36 hours; nobody at home knew, but I was touch and go for that period of time. I didn't even know myself how serious it was, as I was out of it. When a friend of mine, JJ O'Shea, came up from his home in London to collect me, he got a shock – I was like a ghost after the ordeal. If someone had said then that I'd be winning All-Irelands a year or two later I'd have laughed at them.

When I got home, I did an interview with *The Kerryman* and, of course, I managed to land into trouble even then. I mentioned the infection and said I was lucky it had happened when I was in hospital in England rather than being at home – by which I meant getting an infection while at home in my house, obviously.

Of course, the following week there were people in *The Kerryman* giving out. 'How dare Pat Spillane criticise the Irish medical system and Irish nurses' and so on: a long letter from a lady in Killorglin who wasn't happy at all with me. (I will say this: when I made my comeback in a National League game in Killorglin, she was one of the first people to come up to me and wish me well.) So, it was the case then, as it is now, that people misinterpreted what I had to say.

Apart from the infection afterwards, Dandy was happy with the operation, which was a boost to the confidence. When I came home, though, I was back in a system that had no experience of rehabbing a cruciate injury. Dandy gave me some basic direction for the early stages of my recovery, but in real terms, it was a journey into the unknown – making it up as I went along.

I had the weight machine in the garage still, but I started in my bedroom with straight-leg lifts while sitting on the side of the bed, and I didn't let up. I was a different animal then, because the injury made me reflect on what had happened and what had brought me to that stage in my life.

It was during that period that I realised that I had never really celebrated the successes, the victories we'd had. I'd let them go by me. Now I was thinking, 'If I ever win anything else, I'll appreciate it.' What made more of an impression on me was the realisation that once I'd done my cruciate, I was gone. I wasn't a Kerry footballer any more. I wasn't part of the panel: out of sight and out of mind.

Frank King, the county board chairman, got in touch a couple of times, and so did Dwyer. Did my teammates contact me? Once in a blue moon. That was an eye-opener, realising I was yesterday's man in their eyes. No support, no rehab programme compared to the modern system where the strength and conditioning staff will help you recover. Apart from Claire Edwards, the Kerry team physio at the time, who was great to me, I was on my own.

It was a very lonely time. That was where the intrinsic motivation really kicked in, because I was driven to manic levels of training, and I use that word deliberately. Nowadays, a player will recover from a cruciate in six months, but back then, a year or a year and a half was the time frame, if there even was one, given we were in unknown territory. There were no guarantees. I was willing to put in the work, but it wasn't clear whether I could play again. I relied on work – the old Muhammad Ali line about the ones that hurt being the only ones that count? That became my mantra. If I had 12 reps of an exercise to do, I'd really work on those last few difficult ones.

I had doubts. I had the voice in my head wheedling at me: 'You'll never get back. You'll never play again. Why are you wasting your time at this? For nothing?' That voice came into my head when I'd go down to work in Templenoe field. It's a beautiful spot in the summer, but on a cold winter's evening the wind would howl in from the sea, with the rain pouring down … by the time you'd get to lap 35 of the field, up to the ankles in mud, it was a fair test of commitment.

I stuck with it, though. My usual routine would be 40 laps of the field with 10-pound weights strapped around the ankles, which was madness, in retrospect. And I'm paying the price now because I have arthritis in my knees. I doubt at that time there was anyone in Ireland training as hard as me, and I'd do it all over again.

I used that voice, that negativity, as fuel. I'd show I was up to it by running the last five laps faster than the first five to show I could still do it, or I'd rip through the last four or five reps of the weight with more and more force. It drove me.

There was a field across from the bar with a slope of about 100 metres across it. The ground was absolute mud, but I'd do four sets of ten sprints each up the slope. Sprint up, walk down. Sprint up, walk down. Forty times. I learned to use everything as positive ammunition along the way. A little twinge in the leg the morning after training? It's healing away, I'd tell myself. I'd look at the leg and think, 'I'm getting stronger and stronger, I can see it.' Everything was positive reinforcement.

It changed me as a person as well, because I felt from then on it was about me. I didn't owe anything to the county or to my teammates or my supporters or my club: I had done all the work and I owed it all to myself, proving that I could get back and that I'd be as good as ever I was.

Now, when I look back coolly and calmly I realise that I missed the two best years of my sporting life. I missed some of 1981 and then 1982 and 1983, which would have been my absolute physical peak, my late twenties. Because of that, I can say no one ever saw me at my playing peak.

* * *

When I got back, the analogy of the elastic band made an impression on me. If you snap an elastic band, no matter how you put it back together, it'll never be quite as good again, it'll never be as strong. Even though the operation had been a success and I'd done huge training, I still had to re-educate myself when it came to football.

There were certain things that my left leg just couldn't do any more. Before the injury, my left leg was the one I'd use to start a sprint. I used it to turn and twist, and it was my take-off foot. I had to learn to stop doing those actions with my left foot and start using my right one instead. I was 26 years old and I had to change a way of behaving that had been completely natural to me for my whole life up to that point. It took a lot of getting used to.

The other point was I knew my knee was fragile, and that meant there were certain situations on the playing field that I couldn't take a chance with. Forget about 50-50 challenges, there were plenty of 70-30 balls that I couldn't go for; I had to change my game considerably to account for that.

Don't forget that the game was a lot more physical at that time – players got away with a lot more belting, so I had to take that into account also. It all meant I had to read a situation and react accordingly, but that reaction couldn't give out the signal 'This fella's yellow – he's afraid'. You wouldn't last one game if that was the perception. I'd built up my muscles and my fitness was excellent thanks to the work I'd done in the fields around Templenoe, but managing that fear was the biggest challenge.

I played in a challenge game for Kerry against Dublin one evening in Parnell Park, but it was casual enough. The big test came in a county league game with Templenoe soon afterwards. The first one or two of those league games I was nervous enough, but then there was a match against Knocknagoshel, a no-nonsense team who didn't believe in standing on ceremony. They were one of the few teams whose players would cream you but would be genuine afterwards when asking how you were. They played that time in The Mall, their old pitch, which was a tight field with nowhere to hide. After the game, which was as hard-hitting as I'd expected, I suddenly realised that I hadn't thought once about the knee because I'd been concentrating totally on the game.

The pub we went to afterwards for a drink? The Wounded Knee. You couldn't make it up. I could see the funny side of it because, after the torture of rehab, my knee wasn't wounded any more. I was ready to return to the green and gold of Kerry as well as the blue and white of Templenoe.

CHAPTER 9

BONUS TERRITORY

After my operation and rehab, getting back to play properly in 1984 was liberation, particularly after the disappointment of 1982 and missing out on 1983 as I recuperated. (Also, in 1984, I was on the Team of the Century as part of the GAA's centenary year celebrations. An Post issued commemorative stamps with the players' faces. The effect was spoiled a little for me when a Corkman told me he'd bought a stamp with my face on it but he wasn't sure which side to spit on.)

Playing in 1984 was a second chance for me after all the setbacks and being told I'd never play again. It was like 1975 because there was a certain amount of rebuilding with a few lads stepping down. Transition wasn't the description applied to teams at that time, but our team was changing:

John Kennedy, Ger Lynch, Ambrose O'Donovan were coming in. My brother Tom went to centre-back as well, a master stroke from Dwyer to put him there. He was fresh at centre-back, Ger Lynch was fresh at wing-back, and Ambrose was new at midfield, so we had fresh blood all over the field, and that gave the team a spark in the same way that moving Bomber to full-forward did in 1978. We beat Cork and Galway before facing Dublin in the final, and that was special.

The first All-Ireland in 1975 was great because it was the first, and 1978 was memorable because we'd lost the previous two years, and defeat always makes you appreciate victory all the more. But that was one part of my career, and by 1982 I should have been gone after that injury. From 1984 on, therefore, was a bonus, an entire career, almost, that I never thought I'd have – never mind winning three All-Ireland medals, three All-Stars and two Footballer of the Year awards.

When I came back in 1984, I was stronger, fitter and faster than I'd been before getting injured. That injury may have robbed me of two of my best years, but when I got back it was bonus territory.

I got two of my best points ever in that 1984 All-Ireland against Dublin. One came from a misplaced pass out under the corner of the Hogan and Nally Stand and was probably the most spectacular kick I ever took, but I used to practise that kick in Fitzgerald Stadium night after night after night.

And that confidence comes from practice. I'd kicked that ball a million times before I ever kicked it that day in 1984. I'd visualised it with a Dublin corner-back closing in to block me in the last minute of a game all those times in training with Kerry. That's where the confidence came from.

The other point I got in the second half, over by the Cusack Stand. I was miles out but I connected well and after three years of solid weight training I doubt if there was another player in Ireland with stronger legs than me. Add confidence and technique and I was flying it.

* * *

Before I met Rosarii, I was married to the game of football, and that's not an exaggeration. Everything was oriented around training or the game on Sunday and being right for those – having the food right, gear right, sleeping properly. I didn't have relationships because everything was about football.

In the old bar, we had a curtain across the door linking the bar itself and the back kitchen, and on one particular evening, there was music in the bar. Myself and Tommy had a peep out through the curtain to see who was there, and we spotted this good-looking blonde. My speed off the mark told, and I got out to talk to her first; Tommy was more of an endurance runner.

Rosarii was singing 'Follow Me' by John Denver, which became our song. I bought her a drink (a gin, but I let myself down by not bringing any tonic). Frankly, it was love at first sight. The first time he met Rosarii, my friend JJ O'Shea told my mother, 'He's going to marry this girl.'

She was the manageress in Parknasilla and was engaged to be married, though whether she was going to go through with that I don't know. On my first date with Rosarii in Parknasilla, I met a lady at the counter who I asked about Rosarii.

'Oh, that's Rosarii Moloney, the manageress. My daughter is singing at her wedding.'

Great start. Mountain to climb. Challenge accepted.

She claims to this day that she didn't know who I was, but I have my suspicions. What was a help was her complete lack of interest in Gaelic football, so we weren't talking about the game non-stop, but it wasn't easy for her in the early years because I was still playing.

And that meant being selfish. If Rosarii suggested going to the pictures, it was out of the question. I was on the Taliban side of preparation for games, because anything that smacked of enjoyment – a couple of drinks, the cinema – was going to take me out of the zone.

Life was great away from the playing field. But looking back now at the football, the standard in 1985 and 1986

wasn't that great. And by that point, for most of us with Kerry, muscle memory was beginning to kick in. We were winning games easily enough at times, but we also drew with Monaghan in 1985. They were a decent enough team, but we beat them by two goals in the replay. Was it a very good Kerry team? It was alright. We were able to do enough to get by.

In 1985, we did enough to get past Dublin, for instance, but while our best days were over, we had the winning habit. We knew how to win games, how to get over the line when it counted.

Part of that was Dwyer's cuteness, of course. With me, he always let me do my own thing in terms of training when I came back from my operation. I'd have pulled out of certain drills and I'd do others, and he always went along with me because he knew I was doing what was best for the knee and that I'd be right for games. Straight-line running rather than turning and twisting, for example.

One particular drill I couldn't be beaten at, though, was any backwards running or sprinting. I'd built up my quads and hamstrings so much to compensate for the knee that the hamstrings in particular were very strong and running backwards was no bother to me. We'd often do 100 metres backwards across the field in Killarney and I'd win that by 20 metres.

Having said all that, there was one notorious evening that Dwyer made me do the full training session, no exceptions, no dropping out. It was a couple of years later, and I was only just back from my honeymoon, so the reason he put me through the mill that evening could have been to start getting me back to full match fitness after enjoying myself on holiday.

Of course, the other reason might have been the small matter of Templenoe playing Waterville a couple of days later in the championship. My knee was sore after the training session and I couldn't play in that game. Make of that what you will!

* * *

We won the All-Ireland in 1986, and for a change we used 22 players, rather than the usual 18 or 19. We won three in a row, and I'd say it was the best All-Ireland final display I ever gave, if not one of the best games I ever had for Kerry.

Is it a cliché to say that that final showed a team that just knew how to win? I don't think it is. At that time, terms like 'following the process' didn't really exist, but that's what we did. We stuck to what we knew because we knew if we did, we'd get results.

We weren't a great team at that time, certainly – not compared to the 1978 team. Look at the All-Ireland semi-final in '86 against Meath, who were a coming team at that point but were still inexperienced when it came to really big games. They showed that when we got a crucial goal: their goalkeeper and two defenders came out for a long ball into the defence, all of them intent on burying Ger Power, but he just ducked them, let them collide with each other, and picked up the ball for an easy goal. That was the difference in a couple of seconds between experience and inexperience, right in front of you.

The writing was on the wall, though. We beat Cork by four points that year, Meath were as good as us but we fell over the line, and Tyrone were a better team than us – but they'd never won anything and didn't believe they could beat us. It was that simple.

I was on Kevin McCabe against Tyrone, a fantastic athlete with huge pace, and I only got the better of him through cuteness. He was bombing forward all the time and I stayed up in the forwards. The result was we both played our own game, with each of us giving the other the freedom of Croke Park, and that's nearly always a better result for the forward.

If Tyrone had put someone like John Lynch on me, who was more of a sticky man-marker, I'd have had a far harder day out. Here's experience at work again. When McCabe tore up the field and got a big roar from the Tyrone crowd, it didn't bother me. I wasn't thinking, 'Hey, I better chase back and make sure this fella doesn't get any more of those cheers or I'll get the curly finger.' I was confident enough to know that I'd get my chance and that I'd outwit him eventually, but that comes back to my belief in psychology too.

If you're marking someone in an All-Ireland final, then he's at least as strong as you, as fit as you, as skilled as you. I certainly met opponents of whom those things were true, and some of them had the upper hand in quite a few of those categories. All those things being equal, then, how could you gain an edge? For me it was all about playing the game on my terms, not my opponent's. You can't coach it and it's difficult to explain, but this is how I went about it.

First, I demanded the ball. All the time. That was forcing him to defend rather than expressing himself. He had to remain aware of me. Second move? Taking him to parts of the field he didn't want to be in. Into the corner, for instance, where most wing-backs didn't want to be as they preferred being out in open space rather than cooped up.

Third was a gamble, but a calculated gamble: leaving him go off up the field himself once. But if that happened, I had to make absolutely sure I got the ball when that move broke down, and preferably got a score out of that possession. If that happened, you were certain he'd never go up the field again, just in case.

As I've said, Kerry teams were admired by teams in the North – teams who usually realised too late in games that they were capable of winning. That Tyrone team were ready for us and were up for the game, in fairness, and they were six points ahead when they won a penalty.

If they'd gone nine up with a goal from that penalty

would the gap have been too big for us? It might have been, but Kevin McCabe missed it. A lifeline. We didn't panic and started chipping away at their lead, bit by bit. Once that started to happen, their confidence drained away and we reeled them in. But still, it was a lucky All-Ireland. It was the last round-up, but the standards weren't that high all round.

Teams learn from defeat – or they should, anyway. Offaly had learned from 1980 and 1981 and in 1982 were all the better for those defeats. Meath learned from that 1986 semi-final and it helped them to win the next two All-Ireland titles.

You could even say Tyrone learned from that All-Ireland final, because the next time they played Kerry in the championship, in 2003, it was a totally different story. They didn't show the respect they'd shown in 1986 and reaped the rewards. I'd be the first to point out that Kerry people are great to hand out plaudits when we win, and no one better than Dwyer to go into another team's dressing-room and tell them they were great and to keep at it, but none of us is too good when the boot is on the other foot.

* * *

All I remember about 1987 is the clear indication we were on the way down. Larry Tompkins and Shea Fahy had arrived in Cork, and we were meeting a different animal.

Cork had some top players, but those two in particular were great. Shea was an excellent player in his own right, but Larry was one of the greats, no question. He was probably the first professional footballer in the sense that he devoted his life to football – he was certainly the fittest player I knew of at that time. He was the difference. A machine. He could drive up and down the field, carry the ball, score, kick frees, and he drove Cork to beat us in 1987. We drew with them the first day in Páirc Uí Chaoimh – and were lucky to get away with a draw.

Here's where focus comes into it. I'd have always thought of myself up to that point as a very focused player, focused on training, focused on games. Everything else was secondary, and come championship time, I was in the zone.

What really complicated matters was the fact that we were to get engaged the day after the Munster final and we were to go to Dublin for the event. There were no mobiles then, so I remember after the draw ringing Rosarii from the phone in the Office Bar on the quays in Cork to tell her going to Dublin for the engagement wasn't a runner, there was no question. Her reaction convinced me fairly fast that going to Dublin was still very much a runner, and we went.

We got the ring in Appleby's and toasted our engagement in the Westbury around the corner – but I drank orange juice that day. I still trained in Belfield that morning. We got engaged and Rosarii had a glass of champagne and I had some OJ, and I still felt I'd drifted out of the zone. We got hammered by Cork in the replay anyway, despite my efforts to stay focused, which made matters worse.

She probably clocked at that stage the lunatic she was about to marry and she gave me the time and space to train for as long as I played afterwards. We got married in Parknasilla, and we had a great day. Being a country wedding, two rooms were needed to hold the crowd. I had to invite all the players, all the staff in the school in Bantry, all the locals from the area. I often ask people: 'If you had to get married again, how many of the original crowd would you invite? Fifty per cent?' We couldn't invite all the customers from the bar, so we brought them to the afters, and there were definitely people who got invitations to the evening of the wedding who never again set foot in the bar.

* * *

It was worse when we lost in 1988 because I was captain – a great honour on one level, but we were hammered by Cork in Páirc Uí Chaoimh. The only bright light was that Maurice Fitzgerald came through that year.

It was hard to take, because losing to Cork is losing to a neighbour. Beating Cork probably gave us more satisfaction than other teams, so there was more grief in losing to them. You were never allowed to forget it, and I was still teaching

145

in Bantry as well.

And we didn't get on that great with them, either. We had a relationship with the Dubs through Listowel Races, though they were a lot further away. Even with Offaly, we had a good camaraderie with them after 1982, they were good lads. It wasn't that there was animosity with the Cork lads, we just didn't mix that much with them.

* * *

In 1989, we trained harder than we ever had. Dwyer had been loyal to a lot of us and we felt we should show him loyalty in return. People might miss that part, but you're talking about human beings, after all. Loyalty, faith, friendship, trust – they all come into it.

Enoch Powell said all political careers end in failure and it can be true in sport as well. Managers are loyal to the fellas who bring them success. Dwyer was loyal to us – to his cost and to Kerry's cost. We thought there was a last hurrah because every player, every team, thinks there's a last hurrah, but there rarely is.

And it was the hardest year we ever trained, galloping around Kerins O'Rahillys' new pitch. Dwyer was under pressure, we were under pressure, and the answer was to crucify ourselves in training.

In the end, we only lost by three points that year to

Cork, by then a very good Cork team. There was no disgrace in it, but we made the classic mistake: an old team trained too hard instead of staying fresh.

Billy Morgan was a big factor with that Cork team. I love Billy. I couldn't say enough good things about him, and I never had a falling-out with him. He was the engine for Cork. He drove them on, the kind of character who hated Kerry (in a football sense) and a guy the players would die for. When he played, you hated playing against him; when he managed, you hated playing against his teams because you knew well they'd be up for it.

I always got on well with lads like Niall Cahalane, despite everything that happened with us on the field. A gent, a great guy. Players like Jimmy Barry-Murphy and Dinny Allen were geniuses. I was privileged to play once in the Munster team with three other Kerry forwards and Jimmy and Dinny. How did they fit in? You were left thinking about what it would have been like to play with them. There was no shouting about where to pass the ball, it was just there.

* * *

Mickey Ned O'Sullivan came in to replace Dwyer as manager but it was an impossible task. Mickey Ned is a good guy, good thinker on the game, but he was in an impossible position.

Compare it to Brian Cody leaving Kilkenny. Cody did

so on his own terms, whereas Dwyer came under huge pressure in his last couple of years, with the whispers of 'Dwyer must go'. Páidí was right about the Kerry supporters, as I've said already.

Dwyer stayed on too long but, given what he had contributed, I think he should have been allowed to leave on his own terms. Maybe he wouldn't have taken the opportunity to do so, but that criticism of him was very loud and he should have at least been offered that opportunity.

Mickey Ned had studied PE at Strawberry Hill in London and had good ideas, he knew his stuff, but the dressing-room was a cranky one and I don't think he had good selectors with him either. His training sessions were probably too long – a small complaint – with drills that took too long to set up. He was a good coach but he had a thankless task in taking over from Mick O'Dwyer, full stop.

I was dropped, but eventually I was brought back because I was playing well at club level. And I was driven to get back because I wanted to leave on my own terms. That was very important to me. In 1990 I was 34 but I felt as fit as any other player, certainly.

We came to Cork for the 1990 Munster final and overnighted, the first time we ever did for a Munster final. It was the night of an Ireland game in the World Cup and we didn't get an hour's sleep between the lads drinking and watching the game, and chanting when they realised the

Kerry team was in the hotel. (I knew I was gone when they were chanting 'Jacko is a wanker' and I got no mention at all. I obviously didn't pose a threat anymore.)

I was dropped for that game, but I did well when I came on in the second half. Maurice Fitzgerald was centre-field that day and Eamonn Breen, a natural defender, was wing-forward. Ambrose was centre-back. We were rebuilding, granted, but we weren't making progress: Cork won handily the same day.

The following year, we beat Clare by 13 points in Ennis, which was a good sign at least, but against Cork in Killarney we were bigger outsiders than in 1975. It was the poorest Kerry side I ever played in – good club players but not comparable with good Kerry teams.

Still, we caught Cork on the hop. There were no great tactical plans. I was named at full-forward but I roved all over the field instead of staying put near the goals, and Cork never got to grips with us. It was such a shock that in commentary Ger Canning said people would be dancing on the streets of Killarney, the result was so unexpected. That was the semi-final and we beat Limerick in the final – it was a bonus for me to win another Munster medal at that stage.

We had Down in the All-Ireland semi-final and it was the first time we ever did video analysis of the opposition with Kerry. Mickey was ahead of his time with that, but as cranky, grizzled vets we didn't see that. Now it's commonplace, and players get particular segments that are applicable to them and the specific job they'll be doing, but in those days it was just footage of Down winning game after game. They were a good side but seeing them scoring and winning games gave us the impression they were superhuman.

After they beat us, I was frustrated. I was making good runs that day and felt I should have been getting the ball fed into me. That was probably more to do with my crankiness because the end of my career was in sight. It wasn't that I was comparing the lads on that team with the four-in-a-row team, I was having a good year and felt I could do damage with the ball in hand. Down were a good side, give them their due – they showed that in the All-Ireland final afterwards, but we didn't play well.

However, at the final whistle, I had a good look around. I looked at the stands and thought to myself, 'That's it now.' But at least I was going out on my own terms.

That said, if I'd been asked back in 1992 I'd have gone back in a heartbeat. But no one asked me!

CHAPTER 10

FOOTBALL: HOW THE PAST INFORMS THE FUTURE

Questions that I often hear when it comes to football: where are we going; is the standard good; is it improving?

One lazy perception is that I'm always criticising the modern game and always praising the old game in my role as a pundit, so let's start here by stating the blindingly obvious for people who are still too stupid to recognise the truth. And that is, the games in the past were worse than they are now. Inarguably worse, demonstrably worse, much worse. The players nowadays are fitter, stronger and more skilful. You'll get far more higher-quality games nowadays than you did in the past. So, let's just state that to start off.

When it comes to all the great games that Kerry ever played in, there's one common denominator – we lost all the classics. According to the pundits down the years, we were never involved in a classic game that we actually won. All those brilliant matches in the '70s and '80s and '90s were the ones we lost, but the one that's always thrown out in terms of classic games, above all others, is the 1977 All-Ireland senior football semi-final.

As I've already mentioned, it was far from the greatest game of all time. Okay, the weather might have been bad, but if you look at it clinically, the game was basically catch and kick, kick to the opposition, the ball being turned over, mistake after mistake, fumbling, hit and hope. It was an exciting finish, fair enough, but if you stripped away the hype and the excitement and the drama, you suddenly realise it was very poor quality.

I'd describe it as horsing football, very old-fashioned, head down, rooting and tearing. So, let's cut out the idea the game isn't better, because there's another angle to this view of 1977. From 1974 into the early '80s there were really only two teams in the running for the All-Ireland almost every year. If those two teams could serve up that kind of a turkey of a game, what was the standard like everywhere else?

* * *

Change is always happening in sport, and you must embrace it. Evolution and improvement are key, but there's always a question that goes alongside that statement – should evolution be about the improvement and betterment of the game? It's not clear if the evolution of modern tactics is really improving the game. That in turn means taking a look at the evolution of the game in a long-term context to see the effects of previous evolutions.

The first record of a Gaelic football game is in Meath in 1670, and even then there were references to catch and kick, which shows that those are fundamental principles in the game. In the nineteenth century, the game was called *caid*, which seems to have been more of a running game and was very popular in Kerry, though Dublin had a variety of that game in six-a-side *caid* early in the nineteenth century. Presumably, playing space was at a premium.

With soccer and rugby becoming popular, there came a need to formalise the rules of Gaelic football in 1884 with the formation of the GAA – again, two things that seem to be strong from the start with Gaelic football are 'catch and kick', along with an expectation of a 'man-to-man' contest.

The second meeting of the GAA was in Cork. Maurice Davin was charged with regularising the rules of Gaelic football, and he wasn't afraid to borrow helpful elements from other sports. Under his original rules, if the ball went over the sideline it was a throw-in, not a sideline kick. The key to Davin's rules was that he wanted to have a fine, manly game – and that meant you were allowed to wrestle players away from the play. The first game under his rules was between Callan and a team from Kilkenny City, and the scoreline obviously gave rise to concern, because it was nil-all. The first realisation was that referees were needed, and the second was that violence in the game couldn't be allowed to continue.

The history of the first 80 years of the sport was based on two books written on coaching by two Kerrymen. I was privileged to be given a copy of one of those books: *How to Play Gaelic Football* by Dick Fitzgerald, which was published in 1914. Dr Eamon O'Sullivan wrote the other, *The Art and Science of Gaelic Football*, published in 1958. If you read them, you realise how far ahead of their time they both were. Some of the suggestions in Dick Fitzgerald's book are striking. Back then, in 1914, he was suggesting we should have a 13-a-side game, an argument that could still be made. He was proposing that on the basis that it allowed for more skill. Before Davin regularised the rules, Gaelic football was a game based on violence, man on man, but Dick Fitzgerald wanted to move completely away from that idea and made a passionate argument that it was a scientific game. Fitzgerald also pushed the point of view that Gaelic football could be a great game in comparison with its rivals – soccer and rugby – because there was nothing artificial in it. That's a fair point, because you don't have knock-ons, offsides or forward passes.

What was also very interesting was what he wrote about positions on the field. He pinpointed where every player should be on the field and their specific roles. He felt the centre-forward and full-forward should be rovers – the corner-forwards might be scorers but he suggested the two central players should be free men, and that has only come into the game in the last 20-odd years.

Fitzgerald also stressed the importance of the goalkeeper, which is another development in the game over the last 20 years, largely down to Stephen Cluxton's influence, one of the most important players of all time. Yet for decades the goalkeeper was often the worst player on the field, the blocker of last resort. Fitzgerald said the goalkeeper was the most important player on the field, and that 'keepers were born, not made'.

Fitzgerald believed that from a spectator's point of view there was nothing more important than the neat kick on the run, a running kick, but here is where he differs from a lot of modern coaches. He said, 'No matter how great the pressures on a defence, do not make the mistake in the front rank [forwards] of thinking that you will help out your defence by leaving your place to come to the rescue of your backs.' So, under no circumstances come back down the field if you're a forward. (If that message was taken on board we could have had 20 years without the blanket defence.)

Fitzgerald's thinking on training was very advanced. He was an advocate of five-a-side or small-sided games, which are very popular with coaches now. He favoured senior players drawing diagrams on a blackboard to show other players where to go on the field. Sky, eat your heart out: in 1914, Fitzgerald was using a similar mechanism to the lines on an iPad screen. Collective training was an issue in Fitzgerald's time, and was banned eventually, as he warned of training 'too fine' – overtraining, in other words.

The more I read *How to Play Gaelic Football*, the more I find in it. He was warning of the apocalypse of the noughties, decades before it happened: 'We should be loath to copy many of the methods of the modern game ... we should warn of assuming a mechanical character and help to preserve that attractive feature of individuality.'

I look at games we've seen in recent years and 'mechanical nature' is a good description. Fitzgerald felt the most attractive aspects of Gaelic football were high-fielding and well-directed kicks.

Fast forward to Dr Eamonn O'Sullivan, who was a fascinating character himself. We celebrate managers like Mick O'Dwyer, Brian Cody and Jim Gavin, and rightly so, but Weeshie Fogarty's book *Dr Eamonn O'Sullivan – A Man Before His Time* summed him up. As a manager (though that title didn't exist then) Dr Eamonn won eight All-Ireland senior titles over five decades. The only All-Ireland he lost was 1964 (the game my father attended as a selector a couple of days before dying). *The Art and Science of Gaelic Football* emphasised the key elements of the game. Dr Eamonn was very keen on collective training but also took a holistic approach – he didn't mind players having a cigarette or a pint.

His background was in psychiatric care; he was in charge of St Finian's Hospital, so he came with that holistic outlook. He got patients in the hospital to work on the development of Fitzgerald Stadium, which was criticised at the time but would now be regarded as therapy – getting patients out of a hospital environment into the open air to work.

Weeshie Fogarty used to go to his training sessions and always said that those sessions – with quick sprints, skipping, piggy-backs, hand-passing in groups of four – could have been Mick O'Dwyer's 20 years later. O'Sullivan's key belief was in holding position and moving the ball to the forwards. You didn't leave your area but won your battle in that area and moved the ball on. His tactical approach was to reduce clutter and win your position: if you embraced that philosophy, it would kill off the blanket defence, when teams cram themselves into their own half to defend in depth.

Those two men were far ahead of their time in reinforcing what was good about Gaelic football, but they could both also see the potential for problems, what could go wrong with the game. Their books are warnings to future generations.

The great Down footballer Joe Lennon was probably the third man in terms of influential figures in Gaelic football coaching. I went to some of his training courses in Gormanstown, and they were good, in fairness. At them, I saw soccer-style drills for the first time, and Joe's organisational skills made sure they were worth attending. Having said that, Joe made a classic mistake when he remarked in the sixties that Kerry were 20 years behind the times. Ultimately, he got his answer.

In real terms, it wasn't until the late forties that you saw major tactical advances in football. After Kerry beat Antrim in the 1946 All-Ireland, Antrim objected to what they saw as roughhouse tactics from Kerry to stop their slick hand-passing, the off-the-ball movement. Antrim were innovators, with a give-and-go style that might have been borrowed from soccer. You couldn't overstate the importance of drills taken from soccer, right up to my time in Thomond when Dave Weldrick was training us with a lot of soccer drills, in particular drills that emphasised the basic principles of the game – give-and-go, space, width, balance in attack, balance in defence. When you look back now at Antrim, you recognise the quality of their tactics. If they'd beaten Kerry, would Gaelic football tactics have been revolutionised?

The following decade, Dublin came with another tactic: Kevin Heffernan roving out the field from full-forward. But in the 1955 All-Ireland final, Ned Roche, the Kerry full-back, held his spot and Kerry won. If Dublin had won that day, would the game have changed at a faster pace?

Down really brought tactics and thinking about the game to the next level – and to success, particularly against Kerry in 1960. Of course, it just goes to show that I didn't invent Kerry unhappiness about being beaten by a team from the North. Mick O'Dwyer spoke about that Down team being physical, tough, aggressive and quite cynical where they fouled, particularly when it came to the scoring areas. Which shows that tactical fouling wasn't invented today or yesterday.

* * *

One point worth making about Kerry is that for all the perception of the county as conservative in football terms, there's certainly a tradition of learning from defeats, whether it's hand-passing or roving full-forwards. When Jack O'Connor's Kerry side lost to Tyrone back in 2005, he made a point of meeting Northern coaches to see if he could pick up anything to help him.

Decades before that, Kevin Heffernan opened up a new frontier in Gaelic football, not so much in physicality as much as fitness. They moved the game to another level and Kerry recognised that. One drawback Dublin had as a team in the seventies was a lack of prolific scorers, particularly from play. Tony Hanahoe, Anton O'Toole, Bobby Doyle – none of them got a lot of scores, though Jimmy Keaveney was very accurate and John McCarthy chipped in.

But their fitness was a huge asset, and it was one of the first points Dwyer ever made – that we had to match Dublin's fitness and surpass it. We were aware of the work they did. There mightn't have been clips on social media showing them train, but it was common knowledge that they were doing savage sessions. We knew we had to do the same, if not more.

And we did. Yes, the times we trained over 30 nights in a row would make sports scientists shake their heads at the training load, but I think Micko's training methods hold up despite all the advances in training methods and research since. If you reached the All-Ireland final in September, you stopped training afterwards until February. Contrast that with the great idea that is the 'split season', with county action taking place in the first half of the year and club championships the second half. The hidden effect is that the elite players are training year-round, which can't be good.

So, the system was easy to manage. Start in February, peak for September, relax for the rest of the year. The training was laps of the field, and even when he finished up as a manager, training Clare, Dwyer was still getting the players to run laps of the field.

One of Micko's great attributes – which is something that great managers and coaches either have naturally or not, because it can't be learned – was his ability to judge when a player was right. He knew who needed more training, who needed less. When I chatted to Ruby Walsh about Willie Mullins, he said Willie had that innate ability as well. Aidan O'Brien the same.

It wasn't that we were necessarily better than other teams, but we were miles fitter than most of them. It didn't matter a lot of the time how good Mayo or Kildare or Cork were because we had that advantage over them, and it was noticeable.

As we neared the end of the road in the mid-eighties, that advantage wasn't as marked, but from 1975 to 1981 it was often huge. It'd be interesting to see a timeline of scoring in games in those years, just to see how much we scored in the final quarter of games, when the fitness really began to tell.

We also had a psychological advantage over many teams. A lot of Ulster teams were beaten before we went out onto the field, because Kerry were seen as idols up there. Those teams often only realised when the game was nearly over that they were in with a chance. The best example of that was the 1986 All-Ireland final when Tyrone were more than in with a chance – they had a better team than us, no doubt, but they lacked belief.

There were other days when belief was the difference. In 1980, we had a bad day at the office, and Roscommon had come with a game plan to stop us that worked well. Their problem was they didn't have a game plan to beat us, and we got over the line.

Dwyer's tactics were different because he didn't get bogged down in complicated plans. I once said you could write his tactics on the back of a postage stamp, but that was unfair – he dealt in the basic key principles of the game. One, without the ball everyone is a defender, and two, with the ball everyone is an attacker.

But in applying those principles you have to give a lot of freedom to the players to play what's in front of them and make decisions as they go, which is part of the whole 'empowering players to play' phrase we hear a lot now. I think I know what I'm talking about here because I learned these concepts from the all-time master.

CHAPTER 11

DWYER

When my father died, there were no uncles living near us, so I didn't have a father figure or a male role model growing up. It might be an exaggeration to say that Mick O'Dwyer was a father figure to me, but it would only be a small exaggeration, because since I was 18, Micko was a huge presence in my life. I worshipped the ground he walked on.

He was one of my idols growing up and I first met him in 1975 when he brought me onto the senior panel. Not only did he give me my break, but he also stood by me all my life. Always. We never in all our time had a bad word. Never fell out. Ever. There wasn't one word of criticism ever from Micko.

I've always said that my philosophy of life – my view that the glass is half full – came from Micko, because the one thing with him was that positivity that he made you feel. He made you feel special. According to him, you were the best left half-back in Ireland, the best corner-back, the best centre-fielder … he gave off that air of positivity and he was able to instil that positivity into us all. He could make sure you didn't worry about the opposition – that you didn't worry about anything, because the glass was always half full.

That was a positivity he took all through life, and you always felt after a conversation with him, before a game, that you were ten feet tall. Those weren't artificial meetings, just nice casual conversations to kill the time (or so we thought) before heading in to tog out.

Tactics? Did he did he ever tell me he wanted me to do this and that, to go here and there? Not a bit. I just went off and I played wherever I wanted; wherever the ball was I hunted it and ended up wandering all over the field. It was probably aimless stuff at times, but I ran and I ran and I wandered and wandered, but he never once told me to stop. We went from 1975 to 1989 with not as much as a single word of criticism, which is fair campaigning.

Bomber was always his pet. No doubt about that. Bomber lived in Waterville for a while and was Micko's pet project in terms of getting him fit, but I was one of his pets as well. In February and March, when the fatties came in to get fit, I'd be one of the hares brought in to run the fatties. Who were the fatties? Kennelly. Egan. Páidí. Sundry others, depending on how well they'd wintered.

That was accepted as work, though; no one would have seen it as picking on lads. He wouldn't have been hard on players for no reason – not those from the seventies, anyway. Later, he could be hard on newer players: he was tough enough on John Kennedy, critical of him at times. Why? He wasn't one of the 'originals'. Micko would pick him up on the odd stray pass while the likes of us got away with no criticism, really.

How significant was he in terms of what we achieved? Without him, we would probably have won an All-Ireland alright, or two, given the raw talent on the team. But the reason we won eight was Micko. He was the glue that kept us together. He was the conductor, the ringmaster, the point guard.

He had good people with him – the likes of Pat O'Shea from Killorglin was a shrewd boy to have as a selector, as was Joe Keohane – but Micko did nearly everything, the exception being Owen McCrohan, who looked after the massages for players. The selectors weren't there all the time – they'd be present the Tuesday before a game and maybe at a session or two before that, but more often than not, training was us, Micko, McCrohan and a bag of footballs.

The sessions were legendary in and of themselves. Thirty laps of the field. Forty laps of the field. Thirty sessions in a row. Thirty-five. The sessions themselves would probably look outdated now, but lost in that narrative is one crucial fact. He always got it right. Those laps of the field were crucial to build up stamina and character, but he always knew when to taper off that hard training and when to go into the sharp stuff and the ball work. He always had us peaking for the All-Ireland final, and part of that was recognising what individuals needed. Ger Power would be pulled out for a couple of weeks before a game because his hamstrings could be susceptible and they had to be protected. Micko knew it couldn't be one size fits all when it came to training.

He also had a lot of PE teachers on those panels, starting off with Jimmy Deenihan and John O'Keeffe, then myself and Micky Ned O'Sullivan later on. We probably had a greater understanding from our college courses of physical training and physiology and so on, but the dynamic was very simple. Micko was the boss and that was it.

He'd be cute enough to pick up on something we might have mentioned and incorporate it into training, but would he ever ask for advice? No, he was doing his own thing. He'd take on something that might help but the sessions were his. He wouldn't be consulting the PE teachers for their opinions.

He was the shrewdest man in the world when it came to reading a game, to pick up on who was going well and who wasn't. That extended to recognising who was peaking, who was gone over the top – he didn't need someone feeding him stats at half-time to say we'd lost four kick-outs in ten minutes.

We came up against great teams and great players, but he never focused on them. People might find that hard to imagine, but the focus was always on ourselves. It wasn't that Micko didn't do tactics, but what he did, he kept simple. What do I mean by that? He focused on the basic principles of the game. Obvious question: what are those basic principles? I've already mentioned the most basic one of all: without the ball or without possession, everyone is a defender; with the ball, everyone in possession is an attacker. That's total football. At the same time, we were learning those skills with him, Ajax were practising it with the likes of Johan Cruyff, and Ajax are spoken of to this day. But I think Micko hit on total football before them.

It's very simple. It means every player is comfortable in every position – all the players can slot into different positions during the game. That was Kerry in the seventies and eighties – and it's the modern prototype player, where the corner-back is as comfortable shooting for goal as the corner-forward is defending back in his own half. That was it. It was that basic principle of being a defender without the ball and a forward with it. The message we got was a simple one. The mantra was: 'Don't be looking at the O'Neills on the ball.' In other words, play heads-up football.

Those were his three core messages. Without the ball, you're the defender. With the ball, you're an attacker. Heads-up football and don't be looking at the O'Neills. He drove those messages into us and we did the rest.

* * *

Over the years people would ask, 'What's it like to be in a dressing-room before an All-Ireland final?' They'd have been surprised by Micko's team talks. There were no great gimmicks, no throwing medals against the wall like Joe Kernan is supposed to have done at half-time in the 2002 All-Ireland. There were no inspired pieces of tactical genius introduced at the last minute, nor was there much in the way of dazzling rhetoric. There was no instilling of 'the greats have to carry on the legacy of Kerry football'.

One clever move on his part, though, was to say that we had 31 and a half counties against us. That was part of his motivation. Ostensibly, we were playing for our club, playing for our family, playing for our county, but intrinsically we were playing for ourselves.

Famously, he gave a talk one year and his false teeth fell out while he was talking. After the game, someone said that it was funny when O'Dwyer's teeth fell out before the game. But no one else saw it. Why? Because the 25 fellas sitting in the dressing-room were all ready. Physically present but mentally already out on the field. There was Micko with the green jumper and the programme rolled up in front of

Michael, myself and our parents outside the bar in 1960 or 1961.

My First Communion.

The whole family in 1975:
(from left to right) me, Margaret, Tommy, our mother Maura and Michael.

Being seen off by our mother as we were leaving for training in 1984.
(© *The Kerryman*)

Me lifting the Sam Maguire after the 1975 All-Ireland football final,
where we played Dublin. Donal Keenan, President of the GAA, presented
it to me. Worst acceptance speech ever. The team captain was taken to
hospital during the game, so I (as the vice-captain) had to do it.
(© Independent News and Media/Getty Images)

The Kerry team that defeated Dublin in the All-Ireland final
at Croke Park in 1979. Another good day out.
(© Independent News and Media/Getty Images)

At the World Superstars competition in the Bahamas in 1979.
An amazing experience. Showcasing the original Pat Spillane tan.

A proud mother displaying her sons' medals and trophies.
(© Don MacMonagle – macmonagle.com)

The All-Ireland football final in September 1985. We won the championship following a 2–12 to 2–8 defeat of Dublin. (© INPHO/Billy Stickland)

From left to right: me, Michael, his son Cormac, and Tommy at the opening of the pitch in Templenoe.

Finally captured after 33 years of freedom. From left to right: Tommy; my mother; Mike's wife, Fiona; me; my sister, Margaret; Rosarii; and Mike. An unforgettable day at Parknasilla, 26 March 1988.

The 1986 All-Ireland semi-final against Meath. We won the final, and I got Player of the Year. (© INPHO/Billy Stickland)

The day Pat Junior came home from the hospital.
The footballer had arrived – my mother's happiest moment.

Having fun in the back garden with Cara, Shona and Pat Junior.

In the back garden with Shona and Pat Junior – future Kerry footballers.

We had the launch of TG4's *Laochra Gael* series in the bar in 2003.
(© Don MacMonagle – macmonagle.com)

Me and Bertie Ahern at the official reopening of the Templenoe GAA pitch on 26 April 2003, when I was chairman of Templenoe GAA Club. Kerry played Dublin that day. (© Don MacMonagle – macmonagle.com)

Training youngsters in the Middle East in the early 2000s.

Joining the Texaco Sports Stars Hall of Fame in 2011.
A proud moment and a great night at the Four Seasons Hotel in Dublin.
(© SPORTSFILE/Stephen McCarthy)

Another day at the office. I'm next to former Mayo manager John Maughan
and presenter Evanne Ní Chuilinn. Cusack Park, Ennis, July 2017.
(© Diarmuid Greene/Getty Images)

Colm O'Rourke, Joe Brolly, myself and Michael Lyster before the All-Ireland senior championship final between Dublin and Tyrone at Croke Park in September 2018. Simply the best. (© Brendan Moran/Getty Images)

Me and Pat Junior on my final day in the RTÉ studio in July 2022, after Kerry had just beaten Galway. That was magic!

Last day at the office and the first visit from the family in 30 years.
Cara, me, Rosarii, Shona, Liam and Pat Junior.

Pat Junior's first home game for Sligo on 6 February 2022 and our first time
watching him play – a surprise visit and a really special day.

Pat Junior in the Tailteann Cup semi-final between Sligo and Cavan in June 2022. (© INPHO/Ben Brady)

Watching Pat Junior play for Sligo against Wicklow in the
Allianz Football League Division 4 final in Croke Park in April 2023.
(© Tyler Miller/Getty Images)

On the sideline after the match – a magic day for the whole family.

Me and my eight All-Ireland medals. I won my last medal in 1986,
the year I met Rosarii. I had it made into a bracelet – hopeless romantic.
(© Don MacMonagle – macmonagle.com)

Like grandfather, like granddaughter. Time to put my feet up.

them, but they were already ready, even if he was banging a bottle off the table in front of them.

From a very low base he had success elsewhere as well. Success with Laois. An All-Ireland final with Kildare. He'd always say about Kildare that what caught them in that 1998 All-Ireland final – a little like the five-in-a-row – was outside pressure. The carnival there was in Kildare at the time got through to the players. The carnival around Kerry for five-in-a-row didn't get to the players; we had played six or seven All-Ireland finals at that stage. But when it got to 20 minutes to go, suddenly we realised the enormity of what was on our doorstep. And then it got to us.

There were so many simple things that he believed in which carried him through, particularly with Kerry. He was very much a believer in the players, in the squad, and everyone being part of the squad. By doing so – believing so much in the players – he was ahead of his time in the sense that he was anti-bureaucracy, and anti-GAA to a certain extent. I would say he was no great fan of the county board but in fairness he had good guys to work with – Frank King, Ger McKenna – and they were cute enough to leave him in charge. Why fix something that wasn't broken?

But Micko was very strong on the proper expenses being given to players, on having them well looked after. A big steak for dinner after training every night.

He was also cute enough to pick up on the potential for trouble when there was a bit of success early on. The couple of high-profile fellas doing well in those days might have been an issue, and Micko wasn't happy with that. He made sure that any deals that were struck would benefit everybody, all the players, all the selectors, everybody.

Hence the great Bendix deal, which he dreamed up, that showed a few Kerry players in a newspaper ad for Bendix washing machines on the morning of the 1985 All-Ireland. He was a businessman, he was commercially driven. He knew how to make a few bob and he worked out that there were certain companies, even early on, that were exploiting us. They were putting us on calendars and selling them, but we were getting nothing out of it.

And he was ruthless in response. For the four-in-a-row he said, 'We'll have a calendar out the day after the All-Ireland.' On the morning of the All-Ireland final, we took a team calendar photograph in the Grand Hotel so that it could be on sale within 24 hours. Another year he made sure we never had the full 15 in the team photograph before any game to make sure that no one could use the picture for their own ends. Cuteness.

He didn't want anyone making money off the team and he was ruthless when it came to that. He had no problem making money, or with us making money, if there was money going into the players' fund for a holiday. I'd say he realised around 1979 that All-Ireland medals weren't the motivation to keep us going, that we needed a carrot. The carrot he dangled was the holiday. A medal is a medal is a medal. Once you've won an All-Ireland medal you're an All-Ireland medal winner, and no one can take that away. But after that, if it's two or three or four, it's duplication. He introduced the holidays – the Canaries, for instance, and then the big one in 1981, the round-the-world trip. Though, in fairness, the Canaries was pretty exotic for the seventies.

The holidays were great, we had pocket money, nice outfits, we were in lovely locations, and he realised that they were a major draw for us. In reality, the four- or five-in-a-row is a media creation. For us, the motivation of a four-in-a-row wasn't enough; there had to be a super holiday as well.

Dwyer brought in Tom McCarthy, a successful businessman, to help. He owned the Kingsley Hotel in Cork, the Munster Arms in Bandon, the Hillgrove in Dingle and so on. We had a meeting after a league game in 1980 in the Imperial hotel in Tralee.

'How much do we need?' asked Tom.

'£60,000?' said one of us, pulling a figure out of the air.

'Chicken feed,' said Tom. 'We'll go for £100,000.'

We went for that and made £109,000, which was fair going.

We were in a good position to make money, but we also worked well by focusing on three main schemes. That was because Tom McCarthy said no to Mickey Mouse stuff. He focused on two or three big things rather than ten small things.

171

One was the Mayor of Kerry contest, where the various district boards of Kerry – South Kerry, Mid-Kerry, East Kerry and so on – all got a candidate to be elected mayor.

The second was the portrait of the Kerry team, which you'll still see in many of the big hotels in the county. That sold for £100, which was big money in 1981 – you'd have expected a Jack B. Yeats for that price, and it would have been interesting to see a version from Jack B. compared to the one we got. The lady concerned was a very good artist but didn't have the time to devote to individual portraits of each player, so she did a lot of them from passport photos.

The one slight problem when you're painting somebody from a passport photo is that you don't quite know whether the person is 6'11" or 5'2". If you have a look at the thing now you'll see that the biggest and strongest fella on the team, John O'Keeffe, looks like the smallest, while the smallest fella on the team, Ogie Moran, looks like the biggest. My own mother couldn't pick out Mike, her son, in the painting.

Micko had the right idea by going to the wealthy businesspeople in Kerry and asking them to shit or get off the pot when it came to supporting the county team.

The third idea was going North for two fundraising weekends, because the North was where they loved us the most. They saw us as the Manchester United of the sport and were always keen to see us play, so it was an obvious place to go. The first weekend we played a game under lights in Castleblayney on a Friday night, then we played on a Saturday in Antrim, and on the Sunday we headed across country to play another game in Ballybofey in Donegal.

Another Friday night, we played one game in Burren in Down, on the Saturday we went to Carrickmore in Tyrone, and we finished off that particular trip with a visit to Drogheda for the last game of the weekend.

The entrance fee was £5 for each game and we had the gate. The travelling and accommodation costs were minimal because we were all put up in different houses in the counties we visited and we were treated like royalty everywhere we went.

Micko being Micko, though, he couldn't find it in his heart to trust our hosts 100 per cent, so he brought up the late Tom Keane, whose son Peter Keane later became Kerry manager. The apple doesn't fall far from the tree: another one of Tom's sons is now the successful treasurer of Kerry GAA, overseeing a €1 million profit in 2022.

Tom Keane was a great businessman who knew the value of a penny, and he brought up a bunch of lads in a car from Cahersiveen to oversee the gate. They were the ones collecting from the punters – £5 a head, when sterling was worth a lot more against the punt than it's worth now. In terms of crowds, we were drawing 3,000, 4,000 at least to those games, even though the weather was absolutely filthy for a couple of them.

There were other distractions as well. We played Antrim on one of our trips and there was a function that night in a big machinery shed, a dance with maybe 1,000 people in attendance. It was only March, a long way from the championship, and the dancing was an early-season test of stamina.

The Sunday in Ballybofey was a huge event that went far beyond the game itself. Every juvenile club in Donegal brought their youngsters into the ground, there was a massive parade, and they all got coaching sessions with the Kerry players … it was a great event all in, not just the game.

The second weekend was the time we visited Carrickmore, and as far as I can remember there was no RIC barracks in the town, which meant that the guys who ran the town said, 'Kerry are in town for the night, so there's no closing the pubs.'

We drank all night. Literally.

The only downside was that because we were staying with local families, we had to get up for mass the following morning. It wouldn't have done to miss mass when you were staying with GAA families in the North, obviously enough.

The day after that, still full of drink and with little enough sleep, we hit for Drogheda and played Louth. We beat them on the day, but I can safely say most of us would not have beaten a breathalyser if one had been produced. Nearly all the team took a drink and would have been used to lengthy celebrations, but we were suffering so badly by the time we got to Drogheda we barely got past Louth. And of course, because it was a tight game Micko was in their dressing-room afterwards telling them they'd be there or thereabouts in the Leinster championship.

We made a huge amount of money out of that as well, so we were able to go on our five-week holiday – five weeks in 1981! It broke down to three weeks in Australia, a week in Hawaii and a week between San Francisco and New York. We each had £1,400 in pocket money, but everything paid for.

Amazing. But that was Dwyer for you. If people ask me what I got out of football, then that five weeks would be the prime exhibit.

The following year, obviously the five-in-a-row was a big target, but we were also thinking about the trip. Like planning your honeymoon, you're going to consider the most exotic place you can imagine. For the five-in-a-row, we were going to Bali: unheard-of, exotic, luxurious. Of course, the Monday after the five-in-a-row disappeared, a few of us were drinking in Mulligan's of Poolbeg Street, and Bomber said: 'The only Bali we'll get to this year is Bali-fucking-bunion.'

✶ ✶ ✶

One time in RTÉ, I asked Henry Shefflin if he or any of the Kilkenny players were very close to Brian Cody.

'No,' he said. 'There's a barrier, an invisible barrier, and you don't get beyond that barrier.'

With Dwyer it was different. He was gregarious, and there was no barrier. He was your friend, he was everybody's friend. It was only looking back, years later, that you realised in reality that he was no one's friend but he managed to make you feel, like everyone else, that you were close to him.

Had he faults? Like a lot of of great managers with great teams, he stayed too loyal to a lot of us, no doubt about it. He was slow to break up the team and to introduce new players, and there were certainly players in Kerry who were probably deserving of positions on the 15 – fellas that didn't get a chance. That's because of his loyalty, but to me that's not a failing. It's human nature.

By 1986, we weren't a great team at all, but we had added three more medals after the disappointment of 1982, and that was down to Micko. To me, that was his great achievement. He had an ageing team, lads who had a ton of mileage in the legs and new lads learning the ropes. The general standard wasn't outstanding, but that's neither here nor there. He still got out a team that was able to win those All-Irelands.

His last year, 1989, the money was trailing away because I remember going to training and there were no meals, only a sandwich and maybe a bowl of soup. The steak after training was long gone.

The signs were there. In 1987, we went on a trip to San Francisco to play the All-Stars and there was an unspoken acknowledgement among us all that this was the end of the road. The last trip. We knew that, so we had a ball of a time. On the Saturday before the last game, we went on a fair bender down around Fisherman's Wharf. We wound up in the Buena Vista, the place that claims to have invented Irish Coffee, and we missed a function that night, leading to a headline: 'Kerry team snubs function'. All I can say is that none of us were in a fit state to attend, but it still looked bad.

Things got worse the following day when we played the All-Stars in Balboa Park and got destroyed. Real raggy-ball rovers stuff. It was the only time that Dwyer really got angry with us, and he brought us all training the day after, on a minibus up the coast. He found a peninsula and set us a two-mile run out and back: four miles. The winner of the race was Seán Kelly, the county board chairman, running in his sandals. Bomber came second because he was cute enough to stay hidden in sand dunes on the way out and he joined in for the last 200 yards of the return leg.

When the county board chairman running in his sandals is winning a race with the county senior team, you know the writing's on the wall.

That was the team Micko had facing into that last year, 1989, and he crucified us. I've often told people the story at after-dinner talks to illustrate just how much that year took out of me. I was just after getting married and I'd taken over the bar, so the routine was driving 35 miles to spend the day teaching in Bantry, and then coming back home after school to give Rosarii an hour off from the bar to have her dinner.

After that, I'd get into the car, drive 50 miles to Tralee for absolutely savage training in Kerins O'Rahillys, back into the car and home for 10 p.m. or later before working the last hour or two in the bar that evening.

Of course, one of the nights we were in bed, Rosarii's hand came over to my side of the bed, and I snapped back, 'Rosarii, I'm exhausted.'

She said, 'If Mick O'Dwyer asked you to, you'd do it.'

What could I say?

* * *

I knew the pressure was coming on towards the end of his time with Kerry. It's what's good and bad about Kerry. He was the greatest GAA manager of all time, the greatest Kerry GAA person of all time, but people in Kerry wanted whoever was next. At the end he got a raw deal. He was badly treated in the last year by a lot of Kerry people, which was wrong. But that's Kerry.

I felt sorry for him then. He should have been allowed to manage his exit and to leave on his own terms. He was badly treated by lots of people but I wouldn't call them real Kerry supporters. He would never express his feelings openly, but I know he was very hurt that time. Of course he was.

The only other time I think he genuinely was hurt apart from that was when he wasn't appointed manager of the International Rules team back in 1986. He was going to bring me as the trainer. He was really hurt by that, and I certainly thought, of all the snubs, that was the worst – that the greatest trainer of all time wasn't appointed manager of the International Rules team. That was wrong.

I wouldn't be in regular contact with him – or irregular contact, even – but he rang me a couple of months ago as I was going in to Croke Park for a game. He wanted me to know he agreed with me, whatever I'd been saying that week. Up to a couple of years ago, on a Sunday, he'd buy the *Sunday World* in Waterville, drive up to the car park in Coomakista and read the paper there. I know to this day he'd be watching what I'd say and write. Once I criticised his son Karl O'Dwyer, who was playing for Kildare, on television, and I know he was hurt by that. I apologised to Micko, Mary Carmel (his wife) and Karl over that. He didn't say anything, but I learned that Mary Carmel was angry, and I reached out to them to clear things up.

That's why I can say I know him all my life, and played football for him for 17 years, and there was never a cross word passed between us. To the day I die, I worship the ground the man stands on. I owe everything in football to him. He gave me the chance, he gave me the belief, and he gave me the confidence. And then he just left me off.

Should he have been involved with Kerry later, as an ambassador or a director of football or some role like that? Of course, but the problem is that sometimes we're inclined to ditch people long before their time when they could still be useful.

A great man.

* * *

I had other Kerry managers. The first year I got on the panel was 1974, and that was when Johnny Culloty was over the team.

Johnny was a gentleman, an absolute gentleman, but while he had a good share of the young lads who would go on to play for Micko, he also inherited some of the fellas that he would've played with himself. He was a great thinker on the game and one of the greatest brains in Kerry football, an outstanding goalkeeper himself in his day. But he was also the wrong man in the wrong place at the wrong time. For instance, his training sessions were just too easygoing; you could have played a full game after one of them.

Some of his former teammates had too much influence, and some of them were swinging the lead, full stop. One particular fellow, who shall remain nameless, would come to training and say to Johnny he had a bit of a niggle and then sit on the sideline, smoking. That really was the old world of training and preparation, right in front of you.

Micko changed all of that. He changed it in Kerry, and because he did it there, he changed it all over Ireland. He didn't do it all by himself, of course; he'd be the first to say that the raw materials he had to hand were pretty good to begin with. I played alongside some of the greatest men who ever played Gaelic football.

CHAPTER 12

THE MEN IN THE DRESSING-ROOM

When I wrote my first book, I was the first to do so from that Kerry team, and I genuinely thought I was writing an honest book. Unfortunately, some of what I wrote, which I felt was fairly harmless stuff, reasonable comment, was taken very badly by my teammates.

I hold my hand up. Did I break the omertà of the dressing-room, the culture of secrecy? Maybe I did. Should I have criticised my teammates? Probably not. Was I really criticising them? Not really. I've looked back over it and knowing now the trouble it was going to cause me, would I have written that part? No, because I didn't need to write it. Would I have excluded any comments about my teammates? Yes, I would have, because I can accept I possibly hurt some of them, but it isn't half the backlash I got from some of them, which has continued to this day.

After the book came out, I met two of my former teammates and they refused to shake my hand. Myself and Rosarii were at a function in Tralee and the sister-in-law of one of the players started shouting abuse over at us and gave us two fingers. Certain players would have stirred up the pot of resentment against me as well. Over the years, I've been ignored at functions and made feel unwelcome at events. A former Kerry teammate abused me one night at Tralee greyhound track as he passed me.

As I've said before, with the size of Kerry, many county players are teammates but aren't necessarily friends because they live so far away from each other. Other lads lived outside Kerry and you'd see even less of them. We didn't socialise that much with each other. We were on team holidays but after matches I met up with the Templenoe boys, and the other lads did their own thing with their own pals.

Outside of sitting together for the dinner after training sessions and games, were we together that much? Not really. Apart from my brothers, I socialised a bit with Ger Lynch because he was from Valentia, and Ambrose because he was living over in Killarney. But while we died for each other on the field and trained like dogs together, off the field a lot of us were chalk and cheese. I've spoken to them all since, and that bad feeling has gone for the most part, but as late as last year I went into a restaurant and met a couple of players. One of them smiled at the wall and didn't communicate for the ten minutes I stood at the table talking.

People might call me outspoken, but those who know me know I don't have a bad bone in my body. If someone did something wrong to me but they offered me their hand the following day, I'd accept it. I don't bear grudges. That's something my mother drove into us and I took it on board. But I can't turn back the clock now. None of that takes away the respect I have for the men I played with. I regret those fairly harmless comments, but they were an exceptional bunch of players, and an exceptional bunch of men.

They all brought unique qualities to the group. Paudie O'Mahony and Charlie Nelligan were strong, solid, reliable goalkeepers. Paudie Lynch was the most underrated defender we had, a genius who could put the ball on a plate for you. Years ahead of his time. John O'Keeffe was the fittest, strongest, best athlete I'd say I ever came across on a football field. Commanding around the square. A leader. Jimmy Deenihan? All I can say is that if he hadn't been injured for 1982, we'd have won the five-in-a-row. Not one of the best man-markers of his time, but one of the best man-markers in the history of the game. Enough said.

And Páidí. Páidí was a warrior and he motivated us all because he was so charged up before games, he set the standard for everyone else to reach. To win at all costs. The night before an All-Ireland in the Grand Hotel, you might hear a kerfuffle out in the corridor: Páidí, throwing and catching and running around with a pillow, getting himself in the zone. The same in the dressing-room, revving everyone up.

But the key is the mixture. Someone like Paudie Lynch was the opposite – quiet, unassuming – and you needed that blend. The other Páidí was outspoken but they complemented each other.

Páidí was also someone who trained the way he played. You say 'backs and forwards' and people think that's simplistic. I marked Páidí in a lot of those games and he set the tone; if you got past him once, you knew he'd murder you the second time. More than once, Dwyer moved Páidí off me because he felt I was in danger. The upside was, if I was moving well on Páidí in training, then I was ready for anyone.

Tim Kennelly's power and strength was crucial. Traditional, unfussy centre-back, but when the team was under pressure he could win the vital ball and deliver it upfield. He had Tommy Doyle on one side, whose fitness meant he could have been an Olympic 400-metre runner, I have no doubt about that at all, if a coach had caught him in time. What an engine. Mick, my brother, the same – ferocious speed off the mark – which was obviously a help in picking up opposing forwards.

Pace was a hallmark of our backs. They were all good athletes, just like Ger Lynch in latter years. Tom, my other brother, had it all but didn't have the same focus or he'd have been the best of us.

Seán Walsh was the prototypical modern midfielder and would have done well in the current game because he had the strength, the accuracy, the fielding. He was a beautiful fielder, as seen in the famous picture of him catching the ball over Brian Mullins. His partner, the same. Was Jack O'Shea the greatest footballer of all time? He was up there. It's subjective but he's in that conversation. Strong as an ox, a box-to-box player in soccer parlance, he thrived on the big occasions. The pair of them would have done very well in the modern game.

Ger Power had huge pace and was a savage competitor. Hated losing. He was probably the fastest over 50 yards on the team, but that speed didn't do his hamstrings any favours. Dwyer always kept an eye on that, though, and made sure not to overtrain him. Another coach might have let himself down and injured Power through overdoing it, but Dwyer always pulled him first from training, just in case.

Ogie was the brains: intelligent, great vision, great distributor, particularly with the foot-pass, and linked the play fantastically. He played club football with Bomber, with Beale, so they obviously had a great understanding always, and it worked to our advantage.

Egan was underrated, supposedly, but we knew just how good he was. Unreal strength, but above all, beautiful balance. Right foot, left, always composed, never panicked – always a great attribute for a forward. Laid-back until the big game, when he struck. He got the goal that set us on the way in 1978, after all.

Bomber was the missing link, as I've described him. The final piece of the jigsaw. The out ball for a defender under pressure, the intelligent distributor, the big target man. He was a commanding presence, had great hands, great vision.

In the other corner, Mikey Sheehy's skill level had to be seen to be believed, in all honesty. A genius with the ball. I could argue this one all day long, of course. I said Gooch was the best in the game at one stage, and he was when I said it. Absolutely. Was he better than Mikey? I couldn't say that with absolute certainty. If you asked me for my ten best footballers of all time, I'd enjoy firing out the list and Mikey would be on it without a doubt. When you talk skill, he'd have to be included.

At the time he retired, you were thinking as a Kerry person, 'God, we'll never have another one as good as him.' Then Maurice arrives. After him, we got Gooch, and now David Clifford. Add in geniuses like Matt Connor, Peter Canavan … it's good company to be in.

* * *

Our team was a mosaic. Different people, different personalities, different outlooks, different backgrounds and clubs, all pieced together into a work of art, a masterpiece, by Dwyer. The key point is how different the players were. Talented individuals who were ferociously competitive – in games, in backs and forwards, in training sprints – while being different personalities. All the players were very intelligent, which counts as well, and were able to read a game and play what was in front of them, as the saying goes. All the players were leaders. And the longer we played together, the better we knew each other's play. I knew, putting the ball into the left corner, that Mikey would be there collecting it.

But one of the most important points was that we weren't dependent on one player. Even the greatest teams, if you check, have one or two or maybe three players who are absolutely central. With us it was different players at different times. Mikey and Bomber might win one game. Páidí and Kennelly might win the next. If one or two lads had a bad game, there were others to pitch in; you might hold two of the forwards, or three, but you wouldn't hold all of us. And the forwards were all scoring forwards as well – no one's job was to win the breaks or feed the others. Everyone pitched in with a score or two at least.

As a team we lived hard and trained hard, but in honesty many of the players weren't utterly consumed by Kerry football. Páidí was, but he enjoyed himself over the winter like the rest of us. We were regarded as a great team, at times an unbeatable team. In 1978 and 1979 I couldn't see us being beaten, and I'm not being arrogant when I say that: we were a machine.

There's always a feeling when you're part of that, as a sportsperson, that you're invincible. Invincible on the field, invincible off the field. And I think that has shaken us all to the core, the fact that three of our teammates have passed away – Páidí, Kennelly and Egan. Possibly the three strongest men on the team. Three unbelievable warriors. When something like that happens, it makes you realise that you're human after all. You're not invincible.

We were on a magic carpet ride from 1975 to 1986. A special bunch of players happened to come along at the right time. As it went on, that innocence was replaced by something else, a drive, a desire to stay winning and to stay involved. The fear that someone might come in and take your place if you didn't produce – there wasn't that, really, but it helped to motivate the players.

People can compare us to the modern Dublin football team, but I would still think, 1 to 15, that ours was the greatest team of all time. I say that because in 1982 we were playing for the five-in-a-row with more or less the same team we started with, apart from one or two injuries.

Dublin, over their years of success, had two or three coming in every season and used their bench a lot – as they were entitled to do – but that wasn't something Dwyer did.

The best 15 of all time, to me, was the Kerry first 15 of 1975 to 1979. The Dublin team of 2011 to 2021 was a magnificent team, and I have huge admiration for them. But because of the micromanagement by the backroom, we don't really know them. They should have been on every billboard and on every talk show, but we never really got to know them. What is Brian Fenton really like? Mick Fitzsimons? Jonny Cooper? We don't know them.

Our team was accessible and sociable by comparison, but then again, barring a couple of years or one or two incidents, Kerry have always been good with media – even with the Dublin media. They liked to show us looking out over the sea or up the mountains at times as though we were 'the real Ireland'. Was that Kerry cuteness? I think of it more as spreading the gospel of football, though I'm sure there are people who probably think those are the exact same thing.

Did that accessibility, that identifiability, help us? It did in some ways. It certainly helped me to break my amateur status when I was paid to switch my football boots. I went from Puma to Adidas at the behest of the old Three Stripe International, a company name that will ring a few bells with the players who were around that time. That in itself was a nice perk, but the big one was the trip to New York to play as a guest for one of the clubs out there.

* * *

New York is a great town to visit now, but back in the seventies it was like something from another world. We knew it as the backdrop to *Kojak*. It was so exotic. But the football clubs there were keen to get talent over, and the timing was often very convenient for me as a teacher. A lot of the big games were played over the October bank-holiday weekend, which was handy when you were on mid-term break and could make a fortnight's wages, or more, going over to play a couple of games.

That money was very handy. Looking back, you'd be thinking that there was a living to be made out of it, a fella giving you a fistful of notes 'for the kids' education' (particularly when you were still years away from having any kids). But you were also on the tear in New York. No matter how good the exchange rate was, most of the money was left behind an assortment of bar counters in Manhattan and the Bronx.

Over the years, I wore quite a few clubs' jerseys over there. I lined out for Kerry, Clare, Limerick, Donegal and Tyrone as well. My fans in that county may be surprised to hear that I won a New York championship medal wearing the Tyrone jersey.

There were a couple of times when the offer to come over was so good, I went for the weekend. I used to leave Ireland on a Saturday morning, play a game in Gaelic Park on Sunday afternoon, and be on a flight out of New York back to Ireland that night. I'd land in Shannon around six in the morning and be in front of a classroom in Bantry before lunchtime. Slightly jet-lagged, admittedly, but back at work.

Did the clubs get good value out of me? I had the two chimpanzees in my head that we all have, with one saying, 'Big match Sunday, be focused, be ready,' while the other chimpanzee was telling me, 'You're in the wildest city in the world for God's sake, go out and enjoy yourself.'

Overall? I was probably a bad investment for those clubs.

The other great perk of the time was the All-Star tour, and those were great fun altogether. In the early years of the tours you wouldn't be put up in a hotel; the players would instead be assigned to various Irish-American families, usually first- or second-generation. Their hospitality was fantastic. They were delighted to have a sports star from the old country and would pull out all the stops to make you feel welcome, though that led to some odd experiences. I remember being in Santa Monica on a scorching hot, beautiful day, staying with a family whose house overlooked the beach. A gorgeous spot, the sun beating down … and all of us tucking into bacon and cabbage as the toora-loora music blasted out. To be fair to them, they were trying to make us feel at home, but bacon and cabbage was a struggle on a day when the temperature was probably 30 degrees.

They were lovely people who really made you feel at home, and sometimes there was another perk that a lot of players enjoyed. Many of the families had a daughter or two who took a shine to the players staying in the house, and the players maybe took a shine to them, and not just because the daughters, who all seemed to be called Erin or Shannon or Colleen, had a car and were only too happy to drive the players around. Sometimes there might be a romance between the player and the daughter, and there could be scenes at the airport when the tour was over. You could have one person asking how they could go on at all, and the other person saying their flight was being called and they had to go.

In one famous case in the mid-eighties, an All-Star who shall remain nameless had such an experience before coming back to Ireland. A couple of months later, at home, he got a phone call.

'Hi, it's Shannon!'

'Hi, Shannon, how are you doing?'

'Hey, guess what? I have a surprise for you?'

'You do?'

'I'm in Ireland!'

When our man's heart restarted he made arrangements to meet up but he realised after a day or so that Shannon was in no hurry to go back home, so he resorted to desperate measures. He told her he wanted to bring her somewhere really special, a place that meant a lot to him, a place in Cork.

Ballinspittle.

At the time, people were going there to see the moving statue of Our Lady, and the two of them landed in on a night when there were thousands present and taking the whole experience very seriously. After an hour or two, Shannon whispered that she had had enough of Ballinspittle, and Ireland, and she was thinking of going home a day or two later.

Our man had a line after that about Ballinspittle being able to move people, not statues, but we won't go into that here.

* * *

My travels as a player gave me a sense of the world and I've indulged that since finishing up with *The Sunday Game*. I've been to some fantastic GAA clubs all over the world: Abu Dhabi, Riyadh, Vancouver. I never charge. If they're happy to bring myself and Rosarii over, I'm happy to travel and to do what I can, but what this has shown me is that the GAA club is truly the heart of the diaspora.

Naomh Alee in Riyadh, Saudi Arabia, is the one that stands out. Why the name? It was founded by two Corkmen who named it after the river Lee. Saudi Arabia's a strange place, with no alcohol, as people know. But the GAA club, with typical ingenuity, holds its annual dinner in the one place in the country where alcohol is legal, the Irish Embassy.

Anywhere you go in the world, if there's an Irish community, then the GAA club is the centre of it, helping newcomers get on their feet and offering long-time expats somewhere they can meet up. Mind you, none of them have ever flown me the length of the country in a helicopter.

While I was still teaching, I was approached to do a function in Meath. I didn't want to do it because it was on a school day, but they were insistent, and eventually they broke my resistance when they offered to helicopter me up and have me down for school the following morning. I couldn't resist. The helicopter collected me in Bantry, brought me to Templenoe to collect my clothes, set off for Meath, and I did the gig. I was coming back the following day when disaster struck. Fog.

I was due back to finish off my classes and thought I was done for but the fog lifted just long enough for me to land in the playing field in Bantry where the schoolkids were waiting for their PE class. I was able to jump out of the helicopter onto the field and get the class going. Timed to perfection.

Another evening, Rosarii and I were invited to Áras an Uachtaráin by then President Mary McAleese for an intimate dinner with a mix of people, all of different backgrounds, from North and South. A great honour. Off we went. We were welcomed inside and I was asked what I'd like to drink. A beer, please. No beer in the Áras. Wine all around. But wait, check the cellar just in case. A while later, a chap came back with a warm bottle of stout.

Rosarii kept the menu away from me, because I'm a plain eater, but eventually we went in for our dinner. Starter: liver pâté. No thanks. Main course: quail, with the little legs sticking up, waving in my face. Not for me. Dessert: Baked Alaska. Nope.

We were entertained by one of Ireland's top young pianists, and I found it a long half-hour or so on my diet of breadrolls and warm stout. But it was a great honour to be invited to the Áras, for all that. It's a great memory to have.

* * *

I've also had great opportunities with television programmes, such as *Living with Lucy*. Another show that many people have forgotten was *Wild Trials Extinct*, which was based on the premise that you found an animal which was extinct in Ireland, located its last known whereabouts in this country, and then found its current location in Europe.

For me, it was the brown bear. We went to a cave in Leitrim where the last known bear was killed. I could sympathise with the bear: it was so narrow in the cave I got an attack of claustrophobia.

Then I went to Romania, where the bear's still pretty common, to Transylvania specifically, one of the most stunningly beautiful places I've ever seen. Mind you, the Romanian people were the saddest I'd ever seen, they'd obviously been browbeaten by decades of oppression under

Nicolae Ceaușescu. He had owned the old hunting lodge where we filmed. I don't know what went on there when he used it, but it was one of the only places I've felt genuinely unsettled – there was a very eerie sensation in the place.

It wasn't helped by the fact I needed a pee during the night, which meant two problems. One, there was no toilet inside the building, so you had to go outside, and two, there was a bear scratching at the outside of my window, which was a little discouraging.

I learned a fair bit on that trip. I learned how bears are nocturnal in Romania. And how the human body can hold a pee for eight hours if necessary.

CHAPTER 13

PRACTICE DOESN'T MAKE PERFECT, PERFECT PRACTICE DOES

It's hard to talk about myself in one sense, but when I do, I think it should give hope to everyone for one simple reason. I wasn't a very skilful footballer.

I wouldn't have had the skill of Mikey Sheehy or Maurice Fitzgerald, of Peter Canavan or David Clifford or Matt Connor. I wasn't anything out of the ordinary as an underage player or a county minor. I was an ordinary player who worked hard. If there's a simple message, it's that hard work is the answer – no matter what the question is, but particularly in sport. I never could really kick with my left foot, and the amount of ball I'd have fielded over my head was very limited. Defending? Not great.

But there were two things I was good at. I had a good right foot and I had a good engine, and I concentrated on the two things I was good at rather than trying to be a jack of all trades and master of none.

Many years ago Johnny Giles said that players were better off concentrating on their strengths, whatever they were, than on trying to get a slight improvement in their weaknesses – and he was absolutely right. I certainly tried to make my strengths as strong as I could.

Warren Buffett said about business that you should be passionate about what you do and that you shouldn't be afraid, but the key was to work hard. What was hard work for me? Easy –running and training, training and running, running and training. Building the stamina, building the speed with short runs and long runs.

As I've said, I had settled into school at St Brendan's when, after a couple of days, I crossed the road to the playing fields and started kicking the ball in to the goalposts. That defined the rest of my playing career, because every day meant kicking balls in at those posts – for five years I did that every evening. There were always a few lads over there kicking the ball out and back.

The same in Templenoe. That was a time before ball walls, so I often went down to the field with six footballs in

PRACTICE DOESN'T MAKE PERFECT, PERFECT PRACTICE DOES

a bag. I'd kick those at the goalposts and if they went over a ditch into the field beyond I'd hop over and get them, gather the rest and head back out the field to start the process all over again. I started on the 13-metre line, kicking in front of the goal, then out to the 20-metre line and on out to the 45. Then I'd go to the left wing, take shots from all of those lines again, then the right wing. After that, I'd try shots from the corner flag and other difficult angles, anything to test myself.

I had the technique, and I'll repeat it to anyone who wants to listen. It was always left foot planted on the ground, shoulder pointed at the goal, good purchase on the ball when striking – and that's not something you leave to chance, either. When I'd buy new boots I'd give it a couple of days in the house, sitting with the boot in my lap and the ball on top of it, making that shape to help the purchase on contact. So: good balance, good purchase, shoulder pointed to the goal – and follow-through. Hugely important. The follow-through is often the missing part in the technique; if you watch a darts thrower or a shot putter, they don't stop on release. They follow through to the end.

Running was to make myself as fit as I could be, to give myself an edge. The Monday before the All-Ireland final in 1984 my resting pulse rate was 34, the same as Carlos Lopes, the Olympic marathon champion of that year. Because I reached that level of fitness, that gave me a core of confidence. I knew coming into the last ten minutes there was no way my man would stay with me, that I'd wear him down. I always believed I was fitter than the man I was on. He might beat me for five minutes, ten minutes, fifteen minutes, but I always believed I'd get the better of him eventually. Even now, if I look back at clips of myself playing on YouTube I'm rarely in a 50-50 challenge for a ball or trying to win a ball with a marker stuck right to me. Most of the time I'm winning the ball in space because of all the off-the-ball running I'd done.

Was all that training enjoyable? It was. Go back to Gary Player and his saying: 'The more I practise the luckier I get.' That was me. Preparing well and playing to my two strengths gave me the edge.

Growing up in the sixties, my heroes were Mick O'Connell and Mick O'Dwyer. They were from near my own place and O'Connell in particular was a prince of midfielders, just an unbelievably elegant player. Soccer was also very popular in the sixties thanks to the 1966 World Cup, and I idolised Eusébio and Pelé as well.

But if you asked for an overall sporting hero I'd probably go for Muhammad Ali. I remember a cutting from when he was in his prime that I used to keep in my gearbag and I'd see it the odd time for inspiration, because it was a mantra that drove me. Ali said, 'I don't count my sit-ups. I only start counting when it starts hurting, because they're the only ones that count.' I identified with that. When I started to hurt at training that was saying to me: 'Now you're getting the edge, now you're getting into the zone.'

Micko's most infamous training drill was a wire-to-wire – a 200 metres full-out sprint. I'd always try to be winning at the far wire and coming back I'd never want to be passed out. For the last 100 metres I'd be well into the red zone, but I was very rarely beaten because I was pushing myself to the limit. And it stood to me, absolutely.

Other little things helped. I've referred to Micko's team talks, but he gave me and the others so much self-belief that it wasn't true. We were going out to play games brimming with self-confidence. I know I played on fellas who were better footballers, and a couple of them were definitely fitter than me, or faster – but I always believed I could beat them. That self-belief was crucial.

Also, the last game never counted for anything for me. Maybe it was the Kerry culture, or the demands of the Kerry supporters, but once it was gone it was gone. If it was an All-Ireland final we'd lost, I'd be down for a couple of days, then it was gone. By day three I was looking forward to the next year, and setting higher targets for myself. Those were private targets, maybe it was to score more from play, to score more goals, to win an All-Star, to win a man of the match award. Whatever the targets were, it was a matter of raising the bar.

I was highly motivated, but remember that there are two kinds of motivation: extrinsic and intrinsic. With extrinsic motivation, you're getting a reward – money or a prize or praise – but that never really motivated me. For training, games, championships, the motivation was always intrinsic, the personal satisfaction came from a good training session, from kicking 75 balls out of 80 over the bar. Those were the kinds of motivation I got satisfaction from.

A good training session wasn't a matter of rocking up and doing the bare minimum either. Over the years, thousands of people came to our sessions in Fitzgerald Stadium, and they would have seen my routine up close. I would have been there kicking balls for an hour before training even started. Once the session ended, I stayed on for another 45 minutes kicking ball after ball after ball at the goals.

Because of that, it was a bad day if I didn't have an hour and a half's extra kicking on top of what we did in the training session itself. That extra kicking was being done in a place where we played league games and Munster finals, Fitzgerald Stadium, but I treated every single kick with the same seriousness. I visualised each of those kicks as being taken in an All-Ireland final or a Munster final, with two or three defenders coming in to block me down.

In the modern jargon, it would be called mindful practice, but I was doing it 50 years ago. That motivation came from me, not from any external source. That made me responsible for my performance, which was what I wanted.

* * *

As a PE student, while Kerry were taking off from 1975 to 1977, I benefited from being at the cutting edge of physical preparation. A lot of what we learned could be applied directly to our own preparation as inter-county footballers. I remember a study being cited of 10,000 cadets in West Point in the US, where it was found that those whose primary motivation was intrinsic were 20 per cent more likely to make it through training than those with extrinsic motivation.

When I'm giving team talks or addressing schools, I often quote the Labbi Siffre song, 'Something Inside So Strong'. The lesson I'm trying to give them is they can dare to dream and they can make it. Simplistic, maybe, but it's true.

Every team now gets motivation from psychologists and performance coaches, though I think at inter-county level a lot of the bluffers and spoofers are being found out – inter-county management teams are sharp now, they have proper coaches with particular jobs, and the only place left for bluffers is the sports psychologist or performance coach, whatever that is. Having walked backwards across the Sahara, or whatever they may have done, shows dedication and belief, but does it prove that the person involved has skills which can be beneficial to an inter-county footballer? Whichever team wins the All-Ireland in any given year, you'll hear about things they did or people they had with them. People tend to forget that there were 31 other teams in the championship who were trying different things and involving different people as well.

For years we were hearing that managers were putting on a particular video to drive the team on – the Al Pacino speech from *Any Given Sunday*, for instance: the famous 'game of inches' speech. And you heard just how inspiring that was for the lads who won the league or the championship or the cup. But you knew full well that the other team were listening to Al Pacino roaring and shouting in their dressing-room as well. Yet they lost, so what was the value of Al's speech to them?

I met a man during Covid whose son was on an inter-county panel, and during the lockdown the team management was keeping in touch with them online. One evening my man was out in the corridor but he heard the son roaring and shouting in his room. There was a performance coach of some description roaring on the computer, 'You're going to win the All-Ireland! You're going to win the All-Ireland!' and getting the players to roar it back at him. (Newsflash: they didn't win the All-Ireland.)

This performance coach had never played Gaelic games and, it transpired, didn't know who any of the players were, or their names. How could he improve those players? With these guys you might pick out a nugget or two if they come in for an evening. But if they're around for every training session, players get used to them and they lose their novelty.

My issue with such gurus is simple – I believe fundamentally that motivation comes from within. No matter what the sport, star players and athletes drive themselves.

* * *

One positive feeds another. When I rebuilt my fitness after injury I came back and was able to make the two or three dummy runs necessary to create room for myself to eventually get the ball in space. That was the benefit of the fitness I'd built up, and because of that I wasn't often caught or bottled up. The fitness came from the work, and that work builds the confidence, confidence which is also built from the practice. Vince Lombardi, the American football coach, once put it this way – practice doesn't make perfect, perfect practice makes perfect. That was my approach.

I've mentioned the perception people have of me after watching me for a couple of hours a year on *The Sunday Game*. A lot of people also had a perception of me as a player, having seen me line out for Kerry, which bore no relation to me as an ordinary person off the field.

The Pat Spillane on a football field was annoying to opposition supporters, and probably to some Kerry supporters. I wouldn't have won many popularity contests, though I was a good player, and I've often reflected on the reason why. I wasn't a nice person on the field. I was mouthy as a player. The referee Seamus Aldridge once described me in an article as the king of the cribbers. I would have been giving out to the referee, to my teammates – I was cranky because it was all about winning. I'd have given out to the ref for decisions that went against me, I'd have given out to my teammates for missing chances, or for not passing the ball to me. I had blazing rows with my teammates. I wanted every ball, every pass. If they put a ball wide I'd have pointed out immediately that they should have passed the ball to me. I was a horrible teammate, no doubt about it.

Supporters? If they were shouting at me, I'd happily shout back. I had roaring matches all the time with my brothers, Mike and Tom, when playing for Templenoe, effing and blinding each other all day long. But the minute the game was over, that was over. Would all the lads I abused and roared at have forgiven me since then? To this day, in many cases I'd say not.

One day, we beat Kenmare in a club game, which would have been a huge result for us. I got a record score the same day, but my teammates weren't a bit happy with me afterwards. They felt I should have been passing the ball more. Not so much with Kerry, but there'd definitely be lads with Templenoe who'd still be sore because of the abuse I'd give them. To me, it would have been mild enough – 'Fuck it, why didn't you pass me the ball?' – rather than being personal, but there are lads who've never forgiven me to this day.

But great players are selfish. They're cranky. They're individuals in addition to being team players. The obvious example to me over the last 30 years or so was Roy Keane. When I read about him saying, 'Aggression is what I do, I go to war, you don't contest football matches in a reasonable state of mind,' I recognised that. I had a different state of mind when I went on a football field. It wasn't going to war, the way Roy puts it, but it wasn't a reasonable state of mind either. Winning every single ball was the aim. It wasn't aimless aggression, but I could recognise a lot of my attitude in what Roy was saying. I've seen interviews where he has said people describe him as hard or angry, but he's explained that he just wants to win, and there's no point in not going out to win.

Another good example to me would be Johnny Sexton. He has that attitude – Mr Cranky, Mr Perfection – but he is a winner. I'd demand high standards of myself and of my team – to me, that's Johnny Sexton. I don't know him off the field, but I'm sure he's a different person to the player he is when he's out on the field.

The other great example was someone I came to know during Covid, when I saw *The Last Dance* documentary series on Netflix. Michael Jordan is from the same mould. Not popular, and didn't care to be popular, but ruthless and willing to do anything to win. 'I can't accept failure,' he said. 'Everyone fails at something, but I can't accept not trying.' I recognised that in myself. The same when he said, 'I always turn a negative situation into a positive situation.' I'd be in that camp. When it comes to football, winning is everything, and losing is failure. I'd make no apologies for that. But the minute after the final whistle I could switch off. The game was over and what was said on the field – by me or by an opponent – was forgotten. Gone.

* * *

If I'm looking at the little things that made me, family obviously had a huge influence. My father played for Kerry and three of my uncles had All-Ireland medals; one of them, Jackie, managed Kerry in the sixties. That drives you. You want to emulate your father and your uncles, and coming from a football family, that encouragement and support was there. Football was number one.

Diet was one challenge for me because I have a sweet tooth, but I had no problem getting in the zone for a game. No alcohol two weeks before a big game, for instance.

Sleep was an aspect of my preparation that a lot of people wouldn't be aware of, but when I was involved with Kerry, I slept an average of 12 hours a day. Minimum. That meant bed by midnight and then up at noon the next day. Of course, it didn't happen by accident. My mother facilitated that, leaving the three of us snore away for the morning while she and Margaret worked in the bar making sure we had plenty of rest ahead of training that night or the game that weekend.

Sleep is recognised now as a huge factor in preparing players, but in my career I played in ten All-Ireland football finals and I doubt I had a good night's sleep before any one of them. A broken sleep at best. The paradox is I'd be delighted the morning of the final if I'd had a broken sleep. I'd be thinking to myself, 'That's plenty of nervous energy buzzing through me, that's a good sign for the game.' Though maybe that was just me turning a negative into a positive. Michael Jordan would have been delighted with me.

I had one particular trick that I kept to myself, though in later years I realised there was a name for it – visualisation. Landing into Killarney for a Munster final or Croke Park for an All-Ireland, I'd close my eyes for a good 20 minutes and envision the perfect match. First out to the ball, dummy left, turn right, score – everything. I saw myself in every situation winning the ball, scoring, passing – all positive. Pass, move, return pass, goal. I know it's widespread now and I can't honestly remember where I came across it, whether I read it in a book or was told about it, but it worked for me. It was all positive – everything I did worked out right.

Superstitions? I'd always stand in the same place for the team photograph before a game and sit in the same place in the dressing-room. I always tried to be in the same place coming out of the tunnel, third from the front. And I never missed the two bags of Maltesers in Malahide on the morning of an All-Ireland final. God bless my innocence, I thought that was giving me energy for the game, so any Sunday Kerry were in the All-Ireland final you'd see me walking through Malahide loading in the sweets. This was after a full fry for breakfast, by the way. No porridge or pasta. But that was in keeping with the whole year. Every night after training we had a fine steak, chips and onions in the Park Place in Killarney.

There was other fuel, too. I'd have an eye out the week of an All-Ireland for any article that might be suggesting I was past it, or that my marker would get the better of me. I'd use that to drive myself on. And of course, if there was an article saying the opposite, I was a key man or a big asset for Kerry, I'd be saying to myself, 'Yes, they're right,' and boosting myself. Everything went into the pot to help.

On the Sunday morning of an All-Ireland final, the preparation is all done, anyway. The morning of a final, you're hoping to reap the rewards of all the practice. And in that practice, common sense has to play a huge part, something we lost sight of for a while. Close to games? Plenty of short sharp sprints and kicking, kicking, kicking. A lot of wides in the previous game? Then work on shooting for the next game. That's solid, unspectacular, basic stuff – but that's the stuff that works. I often give talks to businesses or to coaches at training courses, and what I've found is that all of them are looking for the silver bullet, that magic formula or saying, the one thing that will make them sit up and say 'Wow – that's it'. The key.

The truth is a lot simpler than that. I often illustrate that truth by reading out an obituary from the *London Times*.

Today we mourn the passing of a beloved old friend, Common Sense, who has been with us for many years. No one knows for sure how old he was, since his birth records were long ago lost in bureaucratic red tape. He will be remembered as having cultivated such valuable lessons as: knowing when to come in out of the rain; why the early bird gets the worm; life isn't always fair; and maybe it was my fault ...

He is survived by his four stepbrothers: I Know My Rights; I Want It Now; Someone Else Is To Blame; and I'm A Victim.

Not many attended his funeral because so few realised he was gone. If you still remember him, pass this on. If not, join the majority and do nothing.

True. And as true in preparing teams as it is everywhere else. You put in that work and apply that common sense for the joy of winning, and the joy comes from that sense of achievement. As Jordan says, from trying your best.

* * *

The joy of winning leads to great times. Times when we'd come back to the bar and the place was rocking after a great win on a Sunday night. Johnny Bán O'Sullivan and Donal Murt O'Sullivan would give us the poems of Robert Service – Johnny would do 'Dangerous Dan McGrew' and Donal would give us 'The Cremation of Sam McGee'.

Johnny's other party piece, though, was 'The Man in the Glass' and I quote it to anyone who wants to know about success and who's responsible for your success in sport, business or life. It was written by Peter Dale Wimbrow almost 90 years ago, but it still holds true today.

When you get what you want in your struggle for self
And the world makes you king for a day
Just go to the mirror and look at yourself
And see what that man has to say.

For it isn't your father, or mother, or wife
Whose judgment upon you must pass
The fellow whose verdict counts most in your life
Is the one staring back from the glass.

He's the fellow to please – never mind all the rest
For he's with you, clear to the end
And you've passed your most difficult, dangerous test
If the man in the glass is your friend.

You may fool the whole world down the pathway of years
And get pats on the back as you pass
But your final reward will be heartache and tears
If you've cheated the man in the glass.

After that, what else is there? The irony is that for decades I was a 'man in the glass' in a very different sense, as a pundit on television.

CHAPTER 14

THE SUNDAY GAME: APOLOGISING TO THE NATION

I got a chance to join *The Sunday Game* because of a racehorse, Redundant Pal. That horse won the Ladbroke Hurdle in Leopardstown in 1990. It was trained by Paddy Mullins, ridden by Conor O'Dwyer and owned by a syndicate of people in the media industry. Tim O'Connor who was Head of Sport in RTÉ at the time was one of the members of the syndicate, as were some others who worked in the *Sunday World*: Seán Boyne, the great Jimmy Magee and Peter O'Neill, who was my sports editor.

One day Peter asked me if I'd ever be interested in working in television and I said I would. 'I'll talk to Tim, he's in our syndicate,' said Peter, and that's how it started, Peter talking to Tim, and Tim bringing me on board. I started with the *Sunday World* in October 1991, and up to now I've never missed a Sunday. The paper has been absolutely brilliant to me, and so has *The Sunday Game*.

The ultimate in life is to get paid for your hobby, whether as a soccer player, a musician or wherever that hobby takes you, but the next best thing is to get paid for writing or talking about your hobby. From 1991 with the *Sunday World* and from 1992 to 2022 with *The Sunday Game* I've been paid to write and talk about my hobby.

You often hear sportspeople talk about the vacuum when you're retired, and the difficulties a lot of former sportspeople face filling that free time. I was blessed: I walked straight into being part of the games again as soon as I was done playing, going to league and championship matches. I was in Croke Park for all the big games, so I always felt part of it because people were reading my opinions and listening to what I was saying.

People ask if I was ever advised or given media training. We weren't back then. We were never told we should do this or do that, say this or that. Never. Basically, you were there to give your opinion, but I always remember Colm McGinty, deputy editor at the time and subsequently editor of the *Sunday World* – a great guy – saying to me, 'I've only got one piece of advice to give you starting with the *Sunday World* – call it as you see it.'

This was 1991, but he said even then, 'I'm fed up of reading newspapers and a player or a manager – or even an ex-player or an ex-manager – and they're asked their opinion on the game and it's 50-50, or it's the bounce of a ball, or it could go either way. My advice is simple, Pat. Don't sit on the fence. Call it as you see it. Maybe you'll be blunt. Maybe you'll have to be blunt, maybe you'll have to be honest.'

I took that piece of advice to heart. I wouldn't say: 'Could Kerry win? It's a 50-50 game.' I'd say, 'Kerry will beat Cork because Cork aren't good enough.' Ninety per cent of the time that would have been a reasonable enough prediction.

I mentioned the Lyne strain in my mother, that inclination to be direct because of the background in cattle jobbing, perhaps. I think that was a bit of the Lyne coming out in me. My mother called it as she saw it and I think I do the same. Anyone who knows me knows I'll call something as I see it. If it walks like a duck and quacks like a duck, it's a duck. I won't indulge in any Hans Christian Andersen fairytale stuff. I'll be honest.

I started in 1992, and as far as I know, it was one of the first live games, Kildare v Laois in Newbridge. It would have been one of the first live games outside of an All-Ireland semi-final or final, which was the staple diet of live action all through the seventies and eighties.

I wasn't good that first day, but I didn't sink, even if I was only barely keeping the head above water. When they talk about influences in RTÉ, and within *The Sunday Game*, you can talk about the presenters and analysts and pundits, but the man who made *The Sunday Game* was a Kerryman, the late Maurice Reidy. He lived and died for RTÉ and lived and died for the programme. And, most unlike RTÉ, there were no agendas with him. He was passionate about television, passionate about good programming, and the fact that he was a GAA man was a bonus. He was invested in the programme and he had a vision for the programme he could see. He was the man who encouraged me.

✶ ✶ ✶

Am I cranky? No, I'm not. I have good craic and I would think I'm good-humoured. I tried if at all possible down the years to use humour to lighten things up a little. But there's no doubt that in the early years I was very critical of a lot of games and of lots of players.

In 1992, I was working on one of the most famous commentaries of all time: Marty Morrissey's on Clare's win over Kerry. That was also the weekend of my brother Tommy's stag in Lahinch, so we had a good few pints in the Ryan Hotel before hitting for Limerick and that Munster final. Different days. I was with Marty in the press box and I did the country a service because, sick as

I was, I remember saving him from throwing himself out, he was so excited.

Down the years, did I see a green and gold jersey in front of me? Did I see a neighbour in front of me? No, I swear that I didn't. Yet this is the perception: in Kerry I'm anti-Kerry, and outside Kerry I'm pro-Kerry. Work that one out. Maybe I've even been harder on Kerry teams because I'd be passionate and want them to win. I would accept that. But have I ever treated Kerry differently? Once, maybe, but I'll come to that.

Take that 1992 game with Clare. Jack O'Shea was still there at that time, but that was as much of a link as existed with the team I played on. I don't think I was that critical of that Kerry team, even though they were terrible.

I was influenced in those early years by the likes of Eamon Dunphy on RTÉ's soccer coverage. You could see him kicking up wreck, so maybe there was a bit of that to our contributions at times. Maybe I fell into that trap.

Our opinion was subjective. Okay, you base it on evidence, but it's still subjective. If you say Kerry will win, that's based on the evidence, but it's an opinion. Of all the years and all the games, the one that I couldn't see Kerry being beaten in was the game in Páirc Uí Chaoimh against Cork during Covid. It was one of the rare times I said Cork hadn't a chance, and I'd normally not be as blunt as that – I'd give them some chance. If that Kerry team played Cork for the following 364 days, Kerry would win all those games, but on the day Cork won. That's what I mean when I say 'subjective'. If I could actually predict the future, I'd stick to the Lotto numbers.

* * *

Early on the *Sunday World* ran a series of advertising slogans around the pitches of Ireland about me: 'Love him or hate him, read him.' I think that put it into people's heads: 'If I don't love him, I hate him.'

I'd often be wrong, and I might meet a fella during the following week who'd say, 'You were wrong last Sunday, Spillane, you bollocks.'

I'd reply, 'Yes, but I'll get paid next Sunday to explain why I was wrong.'

When Jimmy Magee did a stint commentating for a couple of years for UTV, he'd often have fellas asking him to relay messages to me, none of them complimentary. Jimmy tried to defend me, citing my record, but said his efforts rarely got a hearing.

My poor mother wouldn't say much about the programme but the odd time she'd say, 'Pat, be nice now today.' That was enough.

In those early years, we had a ball of a time, as there was no shortage of money in RTÉ. To get film back from a country venue to RTÉ, they'd get a helicopter to land and collect it, and Michael Lyster would head back in the helicopter with the film. After working on the Sunday night programme there was a free bar in the social club, so I'd stay on in a hotel.

I got 30 years out of it, and I'd like to think it was for helping to make good television. If I called it as I saw it, then I felt I could stand over what I said. But I'd like to think that it was fun as well. What's been forgotten about in recent years, with the advent of Sky, is that television is entertainment. At the end of the day, it's a bit of fun. Of the viewers, maybe 5 per cent of people – push it to 10 per cent, maybe – want serious, in-depth analysis, but 90 per cent of the people want to be entertained. They want to know roughly why one crowd won and the other crowd lost, then have a bit of banter. That's why we cracked it with *The Sunday Game* – it reflected what the GAA and match day are all about for the majority of people. It's about fun, it's about arguments and opinions, colour and craic. That, more than anything else, is what I think we gave people down the years.

My career could have finished before I started, though. Maybe it was a good lesson at the time, because I was after getting over the initial nervousness. I was settling in and was beginning to feel I could say anything at all. The Derry–Tyrone game in 1992 led to the only time I was ever reprimanded by the Head of Sport. That isn't a bad record in 30 years, just one reprimand, but at the time it was tricky. It happened after an Ulster championship game, and typical of the time, it was a game of belting and flaking. I was on analysis, and when it came to some instance of fighting, I described the Derry players as thugs. Out of all the remarks over the years, that was the one which drew huge blowback. I think there was a fear in RTÉ that I had libelled the players and had overstepped the mark.

The shit hit the fan. The Derry county board came out to say their players had been libelled and they were going to sue. RTÉ panicked and the following week was a hurling week, so I wasn't supposed to be on. But the Head of Sport, Tim O'Connor, insisted that I come back in and apologise. I wasn't keen on it, but the job was to keep me on message. Michael Lyster was to take me through the apology, and he was bringing me through it, doing a fair bit of tiptoeing as he went, but eventually I had to speak.

'Look, I suppose in the heat of things I used the word "thugs".'

So far, so good.

'I accept I used that word.'

So far, so good.

'But God almighty, if they committed those acts out there, I think they'd be in jail.'

So, instead of a simple little apology, just to say 'Look, I shouldn't have called them thugs', I complicated things even further.

Tim O'Connor called Lyster into the control room and fired him. It didn't last. I was wheeled back for a third outing, but on this occasion I got a script to read and an autocue on top of that. And Tim O'Connor said, 'If you change one word of that script, I'll kill you.'

I delivered the script.

But I was gone. I remember to this day the Monday morning Tim O'Connor brought me into his office to tell me I was gone. In a way it was probably a very good lesson because I was beginning to believe in my own hype. Eventually Tim went back on his decision and I got back in, but at the time I was fired. I got back in via a back door, *The Monday Game*.

The Monday Game was called 'The Blame on Monday' for a while because it wrapped up the action of the weekend with a view to assigning responsibility to people, or at least that was the perception. It was also pre-recorded, whereas *The Sunday Game* was live 99 per cent of the time.

I had a slot to review the weekend's games on the Monday show, and I was working with Caroline Murphy, the wife of Seán O'Rourke of Radio 1 fame. She'd do the script for me and I delivered it for a couple of months. That bland script wasn't my style at all, and people could recognise that; none of it has ever come up on my highlight reel.

Live TV was great: no rehearsal and all dictated by the game, but *The Monday Game* started recording at 1 p.m. and you could still be there seven hours later, re-recording segments because someone had coughed or sneezed off camera. Eventually, I got back on *The Sunday Game* proper, and the rest is history.

* * *

Was it noticeable, getting recognised by more people? Absolutely. It was life-changing. In the early nineties I was talking on television for maybe an hour and a half a year, and later up to three hours a year, but those few hours defined me as a person in the eyes of the majority of people.

He's this, he's that. He hates us, he hates them. Over the years, the longer I stayed on television, I used to think, 'Do they remember I played football at all?' It was only in my last year or two on the show that I challenged the narrative that I was a bollocks or against one county or the other. I'm not that person.

In 30 years, I could have insulted teams and insulted counties but as regards individuals … if I slagged five people individually over 30 years, that would be the maximum. Maybe I got it wrong at times or was too personal, but 99 per cent of the time if I criticised someone or some team, I backed it up with evidence.

What pissed me off were incidents like Liam O'Neill complaining to RTÉ about the show being 'pathetic' while he was with the Leinster Council. In the early days, when it came to negotiations between RTÉ and the GAA, sometimes the stumbling block in the negotiations would be a GAA demand that I not be used on television. Laughable now when you think about it.

Not being a cheerleader had consequences. I remember one of the GAA officials telling me one day, 'You're a disgrace to the association.' Me? I've spent my life playing, for my club and county, I've been chairman of my club. I'm not anti-GAA. I think down through the years that we were fairly balanced as pundits. Certainly, we were critical, but I make no apologies about highlighting people for wrongdoing on the field of play – for dirty play. If I want to say there's something wrong, I will.

* * *

In those early years, being blunt and being outspoken had other consequences. Pretty soon the abusive stuff started coming and in those days that meant letters.

And plenty of them. Rosarii could collect five to ten letters a day. Whether it was lucky or unlucky, I had an easy address to remember, or to guess at. As a result, a letter from Armagh addressed to 'Pat the bollocks, Kerry' dropped through my letterbox.

In the aftermath of Clare being beaten by Dublin in the 1992 semi-final, I said that Tom Morrissey of Clare should have been put off in one incident. I was critical of Clare and of Tom Morrissey, and the letters I got included a threat to shoot me if I ever set foot in Clare again. I must ask Marty Morrissey if that *fatwa* still exists or if it's been lifted.

There were some truly frightening letters, but for the most part I'd come home and Rosarii would say, 'There's a couple today,' and I'd tear them up and throw them in the bin. I wouldn't be bothered reading them.

What I found is that if a person who doesn't like you, or dislikes what you said, decides to write you a letter, that hatred and vitriol can be so bad that it comes out even in the way they write the address. They couldn't just write Mr Pat Spillane. I'd see Mr Pat Know-All Spillane or Mr Pat Blowhole Spillane, Mr Pat So-Called Analyst Spillane or – one of my favourites – Mr Pat Anti-Clare (or Cork, or Tyrone, or whatever county) Spillane. The other real giveaway was often the way the writing would be dug right into the envelope – the person would have written the address with such venom, leaning on the pen in temper, that the letters looked engraved, not written, on the paper.

I got years of that. I see people talk about social media abuse, which is real, but I can say without fear of contradiction that no one ever in the GAA has gotten more letters of abuse, and more personal abuse on social media, than me. Why? Because I called something as honestly as I could. Did I set out to upset somebody? No, I did the opposite. Did I set out to deliberately antagonise this county or that county? No, I just called something as I saw it and because a person was from that particular county, they reacted badly. I saw the rugby and soccer guys analysing players and it was totally different. People can criticise a member of the Irish soccer team and very few Irish people living here might know him; he might never have even lived in Ireland. In rugby it's the same.

When you criticise a GAA player, there are certain reactions you have to expect. People will say, 'Well, you shouldn't be criticising an amateur player.' But if that player is performing on a big stage, in an All-Ireland final, you have to call it as you see it.

The GAA is generally different to other sports. I remember news reporters remarking that when they wrote articles about the Dublin players being caught breaking the Covid ban, their reports drew an awful lot of abuse down on top of them. These reports were political and written by news reporters rather than sportswriters, but a few of them said they never got more abuse for a story. That's the GAA, because when you're on about a GAA player you're talking about the player, the family, the community, the club – it's the whole shebang. It's a wide circle. Criticise a Dublin footballer, or one from Kerry or Cork, and in general it's like water off a duck's back for those players, even if that's not the case for their supporters.

Ulster teams were always different. I appreciate what they went through during the Troubles. I didn't live there so I don't pretend to understand that fully, but to be able to play despite the obstacles put in their way, the challenges they had to overcome to represent the county, the roadblocks and the physical intimidation. I accept that I come from a different background and wouldn't appreciate all of that.

When you criticise an Ulster player, it's a different animal because you're not just criticising the player and his club. You're criticising his family, his community, Catholicism, republicanism, nationalism, the whole shooting gallery. The Dublin or Kerry or Cork fella might forget the criticism, but in Ulster the elephant never forgot. The provincial element was a big part of that – if you criticise a Dublin player, the lads in Laois and Meath are probably laughing, delighted. But if you criticise an Antrim player, then all of Ulster is up in arms in solidarity. I've probably said more positive things about Tyrone than negatives, but that first negative sticks. It always does.

* * *

What was life like for a pundit who's seen as a critic? Here's a snapshot.

In my broadcasting life, I think only once, outside the Covid seasons, I got a car pass from RTÉ. That might sound petty, but a pass would have been handy when I was public enemy number one and going to Croke Park.

That was tough going. I'd drive up to Dublin and arrive at 9.30 a.m., then park on the Clonliffe Road and sit in the car for two or three hours. Why? Because I wouldn't be up to walking long distances with my knee, so I'd have to get there early in order to find a parking spot close to the stadium. So after a couple of hours I'd head into the stadium, my hood up over my head. I'd be the same leaving – hood up and head down because when I was seen, the abuse was absolutely savage. At least I was parked reasonably close to the stadium, though, for the sake of my knees.

Was I ever fearful of being hit? I was struck by Donegal supporters on the Clonliffe Road and it was scary. It was sad, in a way, to be sitting in a car down some narrow side street before sneaking in ahead of the crowds, but it had to be done.

In the early years it was sometimes worse again, because we were up in a gantry at the back of the Canal End. To access that meant climbing a 50-foot vertical ladder. And without fail, if I had been critical of a team for the last 10 or 15 minutes of the game, their supporters would be underneath the gantry shouting up at me, and then I had to go down the stairs to a waiting mob. Did RTÉ ever inquire about my personal security before or after games? No.

I should have gotten security. It was scary. I remember being introduced to a Mayo woman outside Croke Park who introduced me in turn to her mother. She turned around and said, 'I don't like you,' and started belting me with an umbrella.

Another day, I was flying down from Dublin to Kerry after a game in Croke Park and was getting a lift from Ger Canning to the airport but there was a lynch mob waiting outside the stadium for me: Mayo supporters. I had to lie in the back seat with Ger's coat over me so they wouldn't see me.

The year Armagh won the All-Ireland was the only year Rosarii went to the final and afterwards she was waiting for me when she saw Michael Lyster. She asked where I was, and Michael said, 'Pat could be in a bit of difficulty.' There was a mob waiting for me outside the stadium and our car was parked across the road where the Croke Park Hotel is now. We had to get a garda escort of six or seven officers across the road while a mob of Armagh people were trying to get at me.

On another occasion, those Donegal supporters surrounded me outside Croke Park and threw a few punches into me. In fairness, the Donegal county board chairman was on to me later to apologise, but at the time the incident happened I remember running down to the car, jumping in and driving fast down Clonliffe Road. A garda stopped me and said, 'You're speeding.' I told her there was a baying mob trying to kill me and, to be fair to her, she told me to drive away, just to go a bit slower.

* * *

I fell out with plenty of people along the way, the likes of Jack O'Connor (a couple of times with Jack, to be honest). But the first falling-out was with my former teammate Ogie Moran. Ogie was manager of Kerry, but Páidí Ó Sé had wanted the job. The county board didn't give it to Páidí because they felt he might be a loose cannon, and gave it to Ogie instead in 1993.

The match in question was against Cork in 1995. Kerry were poor at the time. As I recollect, Ogie picked Dara Ó Cinnéide at wing-back. It wasn't a good Kerry team, full stop.

I was watching it from Dublin because it wasn't live on TV, but there was a live stream coming in to the RTÉ studio. Myself, my brother Mike and Maurice Reidy were all watching it, and I think it was because the three of us were watching it together as Kerry people that I was getting angrier and angrier. When I went on air, I was critical of Ogie.

I wasn't being critical on a personal level, but I said something like, my mother would have done a better job. It was obviously meant tongue in cheek, but my emotions had taken over from fair analysis, and it spoiled my relationship with him. And I'm sorry for that.

At the time it got so crazy that the following Sunday a priest in west Kerry denounced me from the altar for being anti-Kerry. Is it any wonder the Church is in trouble with the likes of that? The morning after that sermon, the first request for an interview was from the BBC, which gives an idea of the stir at the time.

The relationship between myself and Ogie never recovered. We've talked on occasion but not much. But it was me talking as a Kerry supporter, passionate for the county and disappointed with what went wrong. Not personal, but Ogie happened to be the manager, before he was replaced by Páidí.

With Jack O'Connor it was different. A situation arose in Páidí's last year as manager of Kerry. He was under pressure, as it was clear that the powers-that-be wanted to get rid of him, and Jack was in for the job. Páidí rang me.

We had been to school together and had won All-Irelands together, we shared a hell of a long road. He was a rogue, but I liked him and knew well the pressure he was under.

'P, will you do me a favour?' He always called me P. 'Will you write an article for next Sunday's paper and say I should still be the Kerry manager?'

Out of loyalty, I did, and that was the only time I ever did it. But just to really get in trouble, I pointed out that the last entry in Jack O'Connor's CV had been as manager of the Kerry U21 team beaten by Waterford. A cheap shot. Of course, Jack still got the job, and he's proven to be an unbelievable manager with a great record, very successful with Kerry.

I never thought anything much about it until the Monday after Kerry won the (first) All-Ireland under Jack, and he was in the *Examiner*, a big two-page interview. He didn't hold back. I was surprised, because there's an unwritten rule in Kerry that when you win you don't have to say 'I proved you wrong' or 'I told you so' when you lift the trophy. In any case, Jack gave me both barrels. He spoke about the article in question and how he had been at his mother's bedside in Tralee hospital when it came out and that she died subsequently. He really tore into me. Hands up. I deserved it.

I could accept where he was coming from. Jack didn't play senior football for Kerry and may have felt he lacked the immediate authority a manager would get from that. Plus, he probably felt that the Golden Years crew weren't as supportive of him as they might have been. In that sense, he probably had a chip on his shoulder.

I can accept that perspective. I think Jack got paranoid about all of that but, given I was writing a piece on behalf of an old teammate, he had a point.

The only time I was ever influenced in any way to do something on *The Sunday Game* was the incident when Paul Galvin threw a water bottle after an Armagh man back in 2006 when a few of them got tangled together by the Hogan Stand. Jack was manager.

I got a call from within the Kerry camp at the time – not from Jack himself – but this was the time I was presenting the programme rather than being a pundit, though. He asked me how we were going to deal with the incident, and I checked with the panel. They were quite adamant that Galvin was out of order and the incident would have to be dealt with on TV. As far as I can remember, there was actually a photograph later of the water bottle hitting somebody in the crowd.

Fair enough.

I was the presenter, the man who was asking the questions, and when the clip came on, God knows it didn't make for good viewing. At all. But by a stroke of luck, the clip also showed the Armagh water carrier arriving to get involved in the shenanigans, so when he came onto the field in the clip, just as the panellists were warming up to discuss Galvin's behaviour, I said, 'And look at the water carrier!' They started talking about the water carrier and more or less forgot about Galvin. It was the only time that I would say I was biased. I didn't deliberately intervene and say he was innocent; I deflected the lads to talk about something else. But it was wrong.

In a way, that probably got me slightly back in Jack's good books, but the Jack of recent years is a different person anyway, particularly in this coming as Kerry manager. I have great time for Jack. He never played senior for Kerry, the Golden Years lads were all on the scene, Micko was Micko – a legend, and a legend based in Waterville, which is near enough to Jack in Dromid in south Kerry. All of that gave Jack that chip on the shoulder, but that's what drove him as a great manager: he is a driven man, and he uses that as fuel.

He's changed over the years, though. Even now, in his third stint with Kerry, he's a different animal. When he was Kerry manager first, he had to micromanage. Back then, would he ever have put in someone like Paddy Tally from the North to work as a coach with him, or put a backroom team together with someone like the former Clare hurler

Tony Griffin as a performance coach? No. But he's matured and mellowed. We all do. Jack has realised it's not a one-man band.

It's no surprise to me that he's the man he is because when you talk about rural Ireland, one of the greatest places, one of the greatest communities in the whole country, is Dromid, where he's from. It's a small place in the Inny valley with a small population, but they're great people. I'm not sure you could exactly say it's the first new town in Ireland since Shannon was built in Clare, but it's not far off. They have the Ionad na Dromoda community centre, which they set up 20 years ago, and it includes six houses the community built themselves in 2006, a daycare centre, childcare facilities, after-school care for working parents, three business units and, recently, a digital hub. If every community had that kind of drive, rural Ireland would be much better off. The stuff they do is brilliant, because that's the kind of people they are, and Jack is of that people even though he's now living back in Ballinskelligs.

I like Jack because what you see is what you get. He can be cranky and grumpy at times but when the history of Kerry football is told in 100 years he'll be there, one of the greats. Absolutely.

Over the years, though, occasionally a text arrived from Jack, and I'd be thinking, *Oh-oh, trouble here.* When the time eventually came when Kerry were talking about reappointing Peter Keane as manager or whether Jack should get it, I was very much in Jack's camp. I wrote an article saying this is the man for Kerry football just before he was appointed. That appeared on a Sunday morning, and as usual on a Sunday morning I was collecting the papers from town when I heard the phone beep.

Text message. Jack. *Oh-oh. Knowing him, he's found something to be annoyed about.* But it was a text to say he was over in London and was sitting down for breakfast in the Crown Hotel in Cricklewood when a fella gave him a copy of the paper and said, 'You better read what your mate Spillane said about you.'

Jack said, 'I read your column and I agree with your comments.'

All pals again.

* * *

That relationship between managers and pundits is an interesting one. In my own experience, nobody got on to me apart from that one time about Galvin's situation, and even that was done quite subtly. Outside of that, did a manager or a county board or anyone else ever give me a shout about an incident over my 30 years on television? Not at all, no.

But has it happened to others? Yes, it certainly has. I've seen other county boards contact pundits.

The crowd who were very subtle were Dublin. Any time there was a debate on the dominance of Dublin and how they were the destroying Leinster championships, or the time Diarmuid Connolly got entangled with a linesman in 2017, then either a member of the production staff of *The Sunday Game* or pundits received subtle messages from people close to the Dublin management team or county board. Not from Jim Gavin or someone like that, but there would be a shot fired across the bows: if you're going to deal with this – not just talking games and players but discussing Dublin's financial power or dominance in Leinster – then there could be trouble for RTÉ, or we won't be dealing with ye, or whatever. That didn't happen to me, because I was dealing with my own fan club. And by that, I mean the Ulster counties.

Of all the statements and quotations and analysis, I'll be remembered for 2003, when I mentioned 'puke football'. How did it happen? It was on the night programme, settling down to watch Kerry play Tyrone, and looking forward to it because Kerry were going to win, obviously. But that's not how it turned out. Everyone can remember the passage of play in front of the Hogan Stand, when Kerry players were swarmed and overrun by Tyrone players, one after the other. By my calculations, there were seven frees in that passage of play, at least. If the referee had blown for the first one – or any of them – then the game would have taken a different shape, though that's neither here nor there.

I ended up watching Kerry lose and that belting and tearing at Darragh Ó Sé and Dara Ó Cinnéide, and I was fuming. I remember walking around before going on the air and thinking, 'This is sickening, sickening, I hate this type of football – it's vomit.' I was thinking that I couldn't say vomit, and I didn't. I said it was puke football. Did I bring that word with me that night? Puke? I did. I couldn't say it was vomit, or shite, so I said puke. I also said I didn't want to see a game that had 72 frees – the equivalent of 92 frees in a soccer game or 82 in a rugby game. It was like kids playing in an overcrowded schoolyard. Puke football has stayed with me since. I mentioned it once and never again after.

This sort of football that I saw today will not fill Croke Park. … This game left a sour taste in my mouth and it's not a case of sour grapes because the better team won today but I'll tell you to describe today's football, do you know what I'd describe it as? I'd call it puke football. And it's not a case of sour grapes because the better team won.

That got me into a lot of trouble, obviously.

It was the second time emotion took over and I didn't give fair, balanced analysis. Looking back, it was because Kerry were being beaten. For years, I'd been part of teams that faced opponents who were already beaten because of the sight of the green and gold jersey, Ulster teams in particular.

Even going back to 1986, when Tyrone themselves should have beaten us in the All-Ireland final. They didn't really believe they could, which was the difference.

When you talk about Ulster football down the years, there was a huge respect for Kerry and Kerry football – we were the Manchester United or the Liverpool, and often we were their second team. Ulster teams were inclined to sit back and admire Kerry and let us play football, and it was only when the game was nearly over, they'd realise they were nearly as good as Kerry.

In fairness to Mickey Harte, he came along and instilled a mentality into his players of tearing into the opponents – no respect, don't sit back. And on that day, that's what they did. They tore into Kerry from the start and deserved their win.

I apologised subsequently because, in fairness, that team was a very, very good team. They played some brilliant football in 2005 and in 2008, but that 'puke football' jibe was a tag they never lost, and I hold my hands up for that. They didn't deserve that and I apologise for it. What I don't apologise for is my sentiment on the day – that is still correct, because I saw in that game the future of Gaelic football: a game that was about stopping the opposition and the opposition's key players.

At an early stage, Ulster counties were thinking outside the box – they were looking at innovative coaching in different sports, and the man they looked at was Clive

Woodward, the England rugby coach who won the Rugby World Cup in 2003. His coaching style, which we saw in the GAA in subsequent years, was paralysis by analysis. Conservative, safety first, no adventure, nothing sent out to the wings, just penalties and drop goals for Jonny Wilkinson.

Ulster coaches learned from that. We saw that culminate in Jimmy McGuinness's Donegal. That was the apocalypse for me, the ultimate in paralysis by analysis.

I make no apologies for saying 'I told you what way football was going' because I did. I have no problem saying the games were worse in the past. Modern players are more skilful and fitter, and a modern-day game played between two attacking teams is better than anything from the past. I couldn't put that in blunter terms.

If it wasn't for Jim Gavin, I don't know what would have happened to Gaelic football. Jim Gavin saved Gaelic football. Absolutely. He came along with an attacking kicking philosophy, front-foot football, however you want to describe it. But the football that we had to endure before that is still in evidence at club level, sadly. Safety-first, paralysis-by-analysis, defensive possession-based football is still rampant. That's what I saw in 2003. I was wrong in how I labelled Tyrone that day but I was right in the direction it was going.

When I criticised an Ulster team, I knew I was poking the bear and was bound to get a reaction. I was public enemy number one up there. As I said, going to matches could be hairy enough.

The plus side was that the more I gave out about them, the more they invited me to do after-dinner speeches and the more they paid. I did dozens upon dozens of those gigs in the North, mainly Tyrone and Armagh. The more I gave out about them, the more they invited me. The one thing that I always said to myself was 'Whatever you do, don't apologise. They don't like you, but they want to hear it again.'

In those days in the North a lot of their functions were sportsmen's dinners – men only, dickie-bow jobs, based on a similar concept in England. What that meant, though, was when you looked out from the stage, about to deliver your speech, knowing you were going to get into trouble – it was like looking out at the AGM of the bouncers of Ireland. It was all big, round, strong skinhead haircuts and red faces looking back up at you: it could be a scary sight.

'I'm Pat Spillane,' I'd start, 'winner of All-Ireland medals from 1978 to 1981, four in a row, and 1984 to 1986, three in a row.'

Silence.

Someone would always shout up, 'What about 1975?'

And I'd say, 'That's right. You know why? Because in Kerry we don't count one in a rows.'

The reaction? Carnage. Sometimes a couple of lads would leave their table to come up for a chat and the *real* bouncers would have to intervene.

Joe Brolly invited me to the Dungiven hurling function one time and I went along as a favour, but I wasn't there long when I realised I wasn't welcome – not because I'm from Kerry, but because I was a football guy. I made it out alive anyway.

The Dublin–Donegal All-Ireland semi-final of 2011 was the nadir. Horrendous. The score at half-time was four points to two, with Donegal winning.

That day, Donegal came with a plan, though it wasn't a plan to win. But at the game I didn't know what to say and ended up saying this:

I don't know what to say. I don't know whether to laugh or cry. I can understand the effectiveness of this defensive system, I can understand that they're not in the business of entertainment and I can understand that it's all about results and Donegal people won't give a tuppenny if they win an All-Ireland playing this sort of football, but heaven help us, Michael, if this is the way the game of Gaelic football is going to go because I've seen the apocalypse there in the last 38 minutes.

Remember that tribe in Iraq, the Shia tribe? Well, we've watched shi'ite football. There are people that go the Hague, Michael, for war crimes. Some of the coaches these days should be [sent there] for crimes against Gaelic football.

That certainly got me in hot water.

The following year, I was covering an early round of the Ulster championship which featured Donegal, and when it came to man of the match, I said no player really deserved to get the award. In the end, I gave it to a Donegal player – Ryan Bradley, I think – but very reluctantly.

This gave Jim McGuinness a crusade. This disrespected Ryan, it disrespected his family, it disrespected his club, Spillane hates us and so on. As a shrewd motivator, he had a cause and that helped to keep him going: Everyone hates us, away we go.

That's an occupational hazard: fire out a comment and it grows legs. I remember when Jack O'Connor was stuck with an ageing Kerry team, another comment came to mind. My Irish wouldn't be wonderful, but I remember the beginning of *Peig*: '*Seánbhean is ea mise anois go bhfuil cos léi insan uaigh is an chos eile ar a bruach.*'

I thought that the second half of that quote would be a good line – 'one foot in the grave and the other on its edge' – so I fired it out. I can only guess that Jack didn't approve, even though he's from a Gaeltacht.

On another occasion, an All-Ireland semi-final between Dublin and Mayo, and Joe Brolly was referring to the boxer Amir Khan. Michael Lyster thought he was talking about the cricketer Imran Khan. I piped up with a story from our world tour with Kerry, when we visited Adelaide in 1981 and I was chatting to this girl who said, 'Do you know who

I was with last night?' Pakistan were on a cricket tour at the same time. She said, 'Imran Khan.'

I said, 'If you see him again, tell him you were with Pat Spillane tonight and he has more All-Ireland medals.'

Completely random. Don't ask me where it came from. Or why I told the whole country.

* * *

In terms of highlights from the three decades, one of the events people often remind me of – and which has unbelievable viewing figures on social media – was the brawl between Mayo and Meath in 1996. I gave it a forensic analysis because it was a serious session of belting, but I also tried to give it a humorous touch.

Here Liam McHale arrives, jumps in, and a wonderful gap opens up. He hits nobody at all and goes straight through, but unfortunately the whole county of Meath seems to come on top of him, and the poor man got an awful killing in this incident. All hell broke loose, and it was very unfortunate. The umpire came out at this stage but, in his wisdom, he removed himself again.

Watch Jimmy McGuinness, number eight for Meath, he arrives on the scene. He exercises his right leg a little bit here, stretching I presume, continues on then and he meets Colm McManamon.

Watch him there, he's looking for a little bit of action, he looks around, just tries to trip some fella, runs along and who does he meet, only the unfortunate Colm McManamon. He does a nice little sumo wrestling impersonation here.

Fair play to McManamon, he held his ground and McGuinness couldn't drop him. So, McGuinness leaves McManamon, but it wasn't all over.

In a short while, you'll see he actually comes back again. Look, there's McManamon after finishing, back again. He says, 'I must finish off this action,' and I tell you this, he'd make Michael Flatley eat his heart out because this is a wonderful high leg action here by him – a wonderful stretch in the right foot.

McHale was very unfortunate. He was sent off because he was the tallest and the most tanned, in fairness, but the point I was making was not to take it that seriously. I'd prefer to be associated with those comments than the odd remark like 'puke football'. That's why I mentioned a dating app a couple of years ago in relation to the Ulster championship.

My love-in with the Ulster Championships continues. The best three matches we've got in this year's championship have come out of the Ulster Championship and do you know what I was thinking? If Tinder did provincial championships, I'd be swiping right to Ulster.

Then there was the time I expressed my opinion about the outbreak of Covid in Tyrone in 2021 or, more specifically, the postponement of the All-Ireland semi-final in 2021 because of an outbreak of Covid within the Tyrone panel.

The way I remember it, there were too many things that smelt about the whole situation, and I just didn't get it. Tyrone played a game of bluff with Kerry and they won, and fair play to them. But when the day came for the game, before we went on the air, I recall Ciarán Whelan saying Seán Cavanagh was up to 90. And he was, he was bouncing around, hyped up to the last. I can't say for definite, but it seemed to me that Seán came with a Tyrone message, and I had questions.

'When there's a vacuum of information,' I said, 'into that vacuum comes misinformation, false narratives, innuendo – and that's what you got. And I still have so many question marks – I'm curious, why did so many people at the one time in the Tyrone camp get Covid?'

I'm still curious about that. Did close contacts come to the Ulster final, did close contacts go to an event and socialise together? To this day, that has never been answered. They pulled a stroke and they got away with it. As for my part, I felt the questions I raised were perfectly valid. And I found out myself on *The Sunday Game* what it was like to be the focus of attention.

CHAPTER 15

THE SUNDAY GAME: EVERYONE'S A PUNDIT

A regular question was straightforward enough: what sort of game do we want?

Gaelic football is still a brilliant game, no matter what's done with the rules, if two teams play with the right attitude. It's absolutely brilliant. Asking what kind of game we want is a good question because it makes us think about the sport as a whole. I'm not being romantic talking about the past, absolutely not, but in 2013 I said:

This game of Gaelic football has been infiltrated by a load of spoofers and bluffers, people with no experience, in some cases, of Gaelic football. Fellas with ear pieces stuck in their ears, psychologists, statisticians, dieticians and, going back to what Colm [O'Rourke] said, we've forgotten the basic principles of the game, the catch and kick, and the fact that the game is still won by the team who can score more than the opposition.

That was 2013, but that viewpoint still holds. Bluffers and spoofers were almost the last people I mentioned when I finished up on *The Sunday Game*, come to think of it. And a lot of them are still with us.

* * *

After the 2012 All-Ireland final, when Donegal beat Mayo, I branched into a bit of Spanish. 'There's a term in Spanish soccer describing a player with a killer pass that can unlock a packed defence,' I said. 'And it's called a *desatascador*, and a *desatascador* is a plunger or an unblocker. Unfortunately, Mayo today hadn't a plunger or an unblocker there who could open up that block defence.'

That was lighthearted. The Diarmuid Connolly incident in 2017 got me into far more trouble. He got involved with a linesman in a Dublin–Carlow game, and the incident was covered by us and Sky Sports in detail. It was the only time, I think, that Jim Gavin let down his guard a little, because he referred to what Colm O'Rourke and I said subsequently, though his comments were mostly aimed at me. Jim said:

> *What concerns me is how his [Diarmuid's] good name was attacked. Before we even saw the referee's report, we have the national broadcaster, both Pat Spillane and Colm O'Rourke, particularly Pat, who had a pre-determined statement.*

Where he got that, I don't know. I'd have notes, but certainly not a predetermined statement.

Gavin continued:

> *We saw the rulebook being read out against him on Sky Sports … before the referee's report had been signed off, there was a … not a media campaign, but it got a lot of traction in the media, and more importantly, [regarding] the right he has as an individual in the Republic, I think his good name was certainly attacked.*

What did I say that had Jim so riled up? The night of the game I said:

This is a very obvious thing. Diarmuid was infuriated at a sideline decision, not giving the ball back.

The pictures tell it all. A picture tells a thousand words: clearly going to Ciarán Brannigan, the linesman, clearly putting his hand on the sideline man, clearly pushing the linesman, which he's not entitled to do, clearly with his finger pointed, threatening the linesman.

You prod a bear, you get a reaction. You prod Diarmuid Connolly, you antagonise Diarmuid Connolly, and you always get a reaction.

He put his hands on the linesman, he pushed the linesman back, and a finger pointed in somebody's face sounds to me like threatening. Bottom line, it's Rule 5 – minor physical interference. It carries a penalty of 12 weeks.

I make no apologies on that. It was exactly as I saw it. Dublin didn't like it and boycotted RTÉ for a few weeks as a result. Did RTÉ ever come back to me on it? No, but what was very interesting was what followed, which led to one of the few times that I was ever critical of *The Sunday Game* presenters and other panellists.

The Sunday night after Jim Gavin's comments, Des Cahill, hosting, brought it up with Joe Brolly and Dessie Dolan, the two pundits in the studio. Both agreed that I was overly harsh in my criticism. Dolan spoke first, drawing attention to the fact that I was from Kerry and saying the criticism looked a bit pointed. Brolly then jumped in, and this was the only time I was ever angry with *The Sunday Game*, really. Brolly said:

> *He [me] is a big boy, and he knows what he said. Of course, Diarmuid shouldn't have touched the official, but at that stage the officials had not taken any action in relation to it, and it was in the context of Connolly being held in the way that he was. You have to say, it was like watching counsel for the prosecution.*
>
> *Pat had everything on but his Kerry blazer and his Kerry tie. I thought to myself after, the CCCC are going to act here.*

Des Cahill asked whether Brolly was blaming me for the suspension, and Brolly responded:

> *At that stage, you were expecting that the Dubs could think, that's the end of the matter. But once it had been jumped on – and it looked to me that Pat was reading out a script – and as soon as I watched it, I thought, they will have to go for him now.*

Des Cahill then pointed out – half in my defence – that most of the lads used notes when acting as pundits, and that it was unfair to blame me for pointing out that Diarmuid had put his hand on the linesman. Brolly replied:

> He did put his hand on the official. But when you play it back, and slow it down, and talk of his past record – let me put it to you this way. Imagine if that had been Colm Cooper.
>
> Your first reaction would have been the same: are the officials not going to protect him? There are three men pushing, shunting him at the sideline. We'd be saying, 'Do players like this not deserve protection?'
>
> But because it is Diarmuid Connolly, and I think Pat bought into it, but there's a feeling that it is open season on Diarmuid. I did think it was over the top, I have to say. He is entitled to his opinion, but I strongly disagreed with it.

Dessie Dolan then highlighted the influence that pundits have and said he felt that that night it was pointed towards Diarmuid Connolly getting a suspension.

Ciarán Whelan texted me when that was going on, making the point that it was discrediting *The Sunday Game* because the one thing analysts prided themselves on was giving opinions based on evidence. He said these boys were plucking their opinions from thin air.

Mike Quirke, now a Kerry selector, texted in to the programme: 'So the lads established that Diarmuid Connolly was only suspended because of Pat Spillane's comments. You're having a laugh.' In a list of potentially unfair statements made on *The Sunday Game* over the years, my views on Diarmuid Connolly wouldn't even get into the top half of the table.

As I was watching the lads hang me out to dry that night, I was saying to myself, 'This is wrong.' How can you suggest somebody has an agenda with no evidence, that someone has a Kerry hat on? I was hurt by that. Joe went in boots up, all studs showing. Dessie never backed me up.

The following morning, some of the head honchos in RTÉ were on to me first thing. Was I alright? How was I feeling? They knew it was trial by television. An assassination.

In fairness to Dessie Dolan, I got on with him well as an analyst, and he rang me later that week to apologise. I could understand the boat he found himself in because I was often in that boat. You could be next to Joe Brolly discussing a game when suddenly Joe could bring you down a rabbit-hole you didn't want to go but you didn't realise you had gone down there until it was too late.

Dessie got a lot of abuse online afterwards, and to be fair to him, when he rang he was really down because it was his first real encounter with the ugly side of fame, I think.

Did Joe ever apologise? No. Joe operates on the principle that no publicity is bad publicity. Did we fall out over it? No. I was disappointed with how Des handled the discussion, but he's a good friend of mine and an able broadcaster.

* * *

I was a presenter for a couple of years on *The Sunday Game*. I wasn't as bad as people said, nor was I as good as I thought I might be. I wasn't bad, but should I have been there? No.

The reason I was there was because Michael Lyster was doing two programmes in one day, so they asked me would I present. I said I would and there was an increase in the money, so I was delighted. Michael himself wasn't too happy because instead of being on television twice in the day he was only on once. In fairness, he came around – he's a good guy and wouldn't hold a grudge.

Some of the producers in RTÉ were put out by me becoming a presenter, but you have to remember that RTÉ is a very strange place to work anyway. I remember going one year to the launch of the spring or summer schedule, and what struck me was that it seemed the falsest and most insincere place I'd ever been. Everyone had the sunglasses on their head even though there was no sun. They were all hugging each other, there was plenty of air-kissing, and they were all saying how marvellous they all were.

What I did learn over the years is that loyalty counted for nothing in RTÉ – the big stars would all stab each other to get on. However, the thing with *The Sunday Game* down through the years is that the staff were terrific – the likes of Ryle Nugent, Paul Byrnes, Rory O'Neill were all great guys.

You went up to RTÉ during the week and you saw crowds of people milling around in administration, and there seemed to be millions of them. Then on a Sunday, you'd see the skeleton staff – the youngsters with insecure jobs on low wages, short-term contracts, working overtime to produce programmes.

Those youngsters were working hard, and I worked hard to try to reflect their efforts. Being a presenter, I decided to be provocative, to fire out hard questions and stir it up. Suggesting there were no tactics in hurling, for instance.

That was interesting because people would say, 'You're presenting *The Sunday Game* and you know nothing about hurling.' Now, I played a bit of hurling – I did mark Brian Cody, remember – and probably played more hurling than a few other presenters if you drilled into it. But as a football man, I wasn't a hurling man, and let's be honest, Hurling Man is a rare breed. Hurling Man is very like Hurling Analyst in that he's a snob who views hurling as the greatest team game in the world and sees nothing wrong with it at all. Ever. They're a bit like the lads in the horse-racing industry – they're cheerleaders for that industry, and the hurling guys are cheerleaders for hurling. If there's something that's bad about the game, they tend not to dwell on it. And I can see where that's coming from, because as a sport it's a small circle, and as a result, they all know each other pretty well. But in football, you don't know each other as well in comparison because you're from opposite ends of the country a lot of the time.

I remember the famous row coming out of the tunnel when Cork and Clare started fighting – Semplegate, in 2007. I knew well that the lads on analysis simply didn't want to know. I was presenting so I kept pressing them – Anthony Daly was one of the pundits – and some people were critical of me pressing them. But that's because it was clear that as pundits they were being pushed to have to say things they didn't want to say.

I admired the hurling pundits, they were all great lads to work with, but they were not prepared to be negative, whereas with football the negativity could almost be a starting point. At times with the football presenters, I'd nearly say, 'Look, this game is shite, stop beating around the bush come out and say so.' But with the hurling boys, it was different. They were like chalk and cheese, the two sets of pundits.

Someone like Ger Loughnane was television gold. Great pundit, great manager, great player, but also blunt and well able to call it straight and call it as he saw it. By and large, though, the hurling lads would stroll in late in the evening, and if Tipperary beat Kilkenny it was Tipperary scores, Kilkenny wides, Bob's your uncle.

That was fine until Donal Óg Cusack arrived. And when I say arrived, he would land in very early in the morning with a laptop, and that wasn't good for the others. Whether he was a better analyst or not didn't matter – he had all the gizmos and the gadgets, so the hurling boys had to up their game. They had to come in early in the morning, and that improved them all.

One man who deserves huge credit is Michael Lyster. I couldn't say enough brilliant things about him because to me Michael Lyster was the man who made *The Sunday Game* sing. Look at some of today's presenters, where everything's rehearsed and scripted, it's question, answer, question, answer.

Then you think back to the really great ones. I did *The Late Late Show* with Gay Byrne who was so good as a host, so skilled, that he'd have you gone down the pathway he wanted you to go even if you didn't want to. That was the level Lyster was at. No agenda. No script other than the links. Questions written down? None. Notes? Zero. And yet he was coolness personified on some of the biggest live shows RTÉ ever broadcast. He'd never repeat a question. He made it look easy, and that's the hardest thing of all – to make a hugely difficult job look like a walk in the park.

The fact that the pundits had a relationship with him was good. We could have a few pints together and he was a good character. One of his key strengths was that he knew what made good television. When you know somebody and you're really close to them, you've been out with them and socialised together, then you know what buttons to push. You know what makes them tick. You can tell what makes them angry and what will bring out their funny side. Lyster knew all those buttons with every pundit that came in.

Above all, he knew when to let things go. He could recognise in the moment that something was taking off in the discussion and he got out of the way and let lads get on with it, which is a rarer talent than you might think. That was instinctive. It wasn't part of any training but something he recognised as it was happening and could help. If a good debate meant scrapping a planned piece of analysis, fine if it was good TV. That's why he was brilliant. Various pundits contributed over the years, absolutely, but he was always the conductor and without a good conductor the orchestra is useless.

Did the public take him for granted? I think so, because he made it look so easy. He was completely unflappable. No temper, no histrionics. I never saw him lose his cool or get angry because of something that came up or went wrong during a broadcast. The beauty of his performance was that he wasn't trying to be front and centre. He didn't want to be taking up the screen, he just hopped a ball for debate – sometimes a grenade rather than a ball – and then sat back to leave us at it with the referee's whistle kept in his back pocket. And we flaked away.

Myself, Colm O'Rourke and Brolly were good television with Lyster wrangling us. The sad part is that we were still good television when somebody decided we weren't working together anymore. We were three very different characters, with little enough in common with each other.

I don't think I ever socialised with O'Rourke. Did I know him? No. We always slagged O'Rourke about the fact that he socialised at a level far above ours, in the enclosure at Royal Ascot or with Jim Bolger and so on. Shrewd, cool, calculating, very dry sense of humour – you knew with him the joke was on its way, it was just that it might come in two hours. He was supposedly cooler and calmer than us, the voice of reason on the panel. In reality, he got away with murder. He said some things that would have had Brolly or me in the height of trouble if we'd come out with them. But he was the counter to us in the public eye – there to balance out the others who were losing the run of themselves. That's what made the chemistry of the team.

Then there was Joe. Joe was great television. Is great television. He's unique. An entertainer. He's box office. Certainly, some of the skirmishes myself and Joe had over the years were box office. I used to always feel, though, that

Joe had an inferiority complex because he had one All-Ireland medal, and O'Rourke and I had more than him. Whether because of that or for other reasons, I felt he needed to make himself the centre of attention.

Unlike Sky or other channels, we didn't do rehearsals or run-throughs. There was no discussion of what questions might come up, and definitely no 'You say this and then I'll say that' among the pundits. We went on air and it was like going on a magic carpet ride or a rollercoaster, because you didn't know where you were going to end up.

But Joe liked to be the centre of attention. There was a bit of a child in him, because during the show he'd be pulling at Michael Lyster's trousers or he'd be pushing in: 'Ask me the first question, ask me the first question.'

One of my problems on TV would be talking too much, and Joe would be pissed off with that. Even if I was making the most amazing point ever made about Gaelic football in the history of television, Joe would be yawning. Or he'd be putting his hands behind his head. Or rolling his hand in the 'wind up' signal, to show that I was taking too long. He could be infuriating. Annoying, though you wouldn't ever really fall out with him.

But he was a barrister, and he always brought his barrister head into the studio. If I said 'up', he'd say 'down', and if I said 'west' then he'd say 'east'. The argument could be me saying Kerry are the best team and Joe disagreeing, saying Cork are the best, and then we'd go to a commercial break. We'd come back after the break and Joe could start explaining why Kerry were the best team in the country, the exact opposite argument to what he had been saying two minutes earlier. That wouldn't bother him. He's a brilliant barrister, very intelligent, a talented wordsmith. He's used to arguments and he's witty.

For 'unglamorous' games it might be a slightly different dynamic. If we were to discuss Longford v Wexford after the commercial break, I'd slag Joe during the break and tell him to take the first question about the Longford forward line – he might say, 'Give me a name or two,' and I'd fire a couple out to him. Then, as we came back from commercial, I'd tell him the two lads didn't even exist. Not a tap out of him – he'd still provide three minutes of analysis, no bother.

Joe would talk away about the game, and he wouldn't even know who the players were. That's his brilliance. I'd come in with pages of notes and stats and so on. Joe would come in, sit down and borrow a sheet of paper and suddenly start writing a couple of things before giving a performance.

In his last appearance on *The Sunday Game*, at one point he wrote a name. Typical enough: on the way in to the game it was customary for him to have met somebody, usually somebody really well-known – Michael D. Higgins, or Bertie Ahern, or the Pope. That person would always have said to keep up the good work.

It was handy that he always met somebody very important on the way up to the stadium that would talk to him and give him enough material to keep him going for three or four minutes without having to go into too much detail about the game. But on that last appearance, when he wrote a name down, I asked who it was. It was the guy that used to be outside the dressing-room door for the Dublin team, apparently.

So, instead of a match preview Joe said he was talking to this man, so he had a Dublin story, like he'd never heard Jim Gavin in all his years as Dublin manager roaring or screaming in the dressing-room.

Great story. Was the name he gave the name of the man outside the dressing-room? Who knows. Was there any truth to the story? Who cares! What it meant was that Joe had occupied four minutes of screen time and we were up and running.

Down through the years, we had plenty of different arguments about every subject under the sun. If it was the Sunday of an All-Ireland final and you said, 'Well, today's Sunday,' if Joe was in the mood, he'd reply with 'No, it's not Sunday because, technically speaking, it's still Saturday in some parts of eastern Siberia.'

A lot of people probably remember the night we had a big argument about Colm Cooper. A little background: at the start of 2022, Joe wrote an article stating that Darren McCurry of Tyrone was the best footballer in Ireland. At the end of the year, he wrote another article stating David Clifford of Kerry was the best footballer in Ireland.

You just have to take a step back – to me, Darren McCurry wasn't even the best footballer in Tyrone – and hang on a second. If you're arguing and someone says Michelangelo was the best painter ever, or Skellig Rock is the most beautiful place in Ireland, even if you have an alternative view, you'll probably acknowledge at least that Michelangelo was a great painter and Skellig Rock is a beautiful place. But with Gooch, Joe's angle was that Gooch was a choker, and with all he'd scored, he had needed to do it in Croke Park, that that's the place to perform.

I said there were two categories of people in the world: the people who don't know, and that was me; and people who don't know they don't know, and that was Joe. Gooch was the best footballer of the time and one of the greatest footballers of all time, and to give Joe credit, he'd argue against that, up and down, and give a good account of himself doing so.

Then there was the day he got into trouble about Marty Morrissey. That day *The Sunday Game* was being broadcast from Thurles where there was a hurling game, which meant the featured football game in the Ulster championship was being shown on a screen in Thurles. Joe asked the floor manager about certain words and whether they could be used on air or not, and eventually he said the game was as ugly as Marty Morrissey.

I'd say that it didn't strike Joe that he had insulted Marty. Marty was very upset, and RTÉ got on to Joe, but he still didn't get what he'd done. He apologised somewhat reluctantly to Marty but – and this is the way he operates – his joke always to Marty in subsequent years was to say, 'I've made you famous, I've given you more publicity and made you famous.'

The final day that Brolly was on was the All-Ireland final of 2019, the game in which Johnny Cooper was sent off. Joe, Ciarán Whelan and myself were on – the first and only time that people said I was the voice of reason.

Joe was wrong on that occasion. David Gough was the referee and made the right call, and I said as much. Joe disagreed and was adamant that he was right, and that Gough was wrong. Ciarán Whelan, who's a very calm guy, a very good analyst and a very good guy overall, got sucked into Joe's game – *this was a conspiracy, this was all wrong.*

Joe was talking over me and he was tapping me, and I know that Joanne Cantwell, who was the presenter, was very cross with him over the way he was interrupting people and hitting me on the leg. But Joe was cranky that day. He was cranky when he arrived at the studio, full stop. He wasn't happy with his VT piece, he was just cranky. But he got that call wrong, full stop.

In all honesty, though, I think Joe getting the sack that time saved my job. I think I got another two years out of it as a result. Would I like to work with Joe again at some point? Of course – those were great years.

Regarding the rest of the pundits, I think people get the impression that Seán Cavanagh is representing Ulster football on the show. I never really got on with him and wouldn't regard him as a particularly close friend.

Kevin McStay is a good operator, very sharp, very analytical, and he's very good on the rules, which is a great asset on a live show. I didn't work that much with Tomás Ó Sé or with Gooch, they'd tend to keep pundits from the same county apart on shows for obvious enough reasons.

A lot of new people have come in. One of the first times I said to myself, 'This is wrong, I think we're going the wrong way with this,' was the period of a year or two of lads dressing up … there was a night Tomás appeared in a dickie bow. All of that eventually became absurd to me. The lads were getting clothes from various companies and would publicise that fact in tweets after the show – small potatoes when you see what came out about RTÉ since. I really thought that was the first time there was a serious dumbing-down. By looking at the clothes and paying attention to those, you couldn't be paying attention to what the pundits were actually saying. I thought that was stupid.

Social media is also very important to a lot of pundits. You could see it during the show – the minute there'd be an ad break, or after the show, a lot of them would fish out the phone immediately to get a handle on the Twitter reaction to their comments – Joe Brolly in particular. I can remember evenings Joe would have the phone out and be saying, 'Jesus, there's some reaction here to that comment.' I'd never be interested in that.

* * *

Another key development was the arrival of Sky Sports into the market, which was a kick up the backside for RTÉ. In terms of production values, RTÉ went up a few notches because it had to. We introduced more gizmos and gadgets, more analysis and deeper analysis, which was very good. The show definitely improved as a result. But if there's a criticism I have of the way *The Sunday Game* went, it was that instead of believing in what we were good at, and remembering what we were good at, we got obsessed with looking at what Sky were doing. We began to believe we should be doing that stuff as well.

I've said before that about 10 per cent of people want deep-dive analysis, and 90 per cent want a general chit-chat and a bit of craic. When you compare Sky analysis and *The Sunday Game* analysis, I come back to the analogy of fast food, with Sky and the other satellite sports channels as the fast-food joints. If you're hungry and you want a burger, then you go to a burger joint. You know what you're going to get: the template is the same, the quality is the same, the burger is excellent, and it satisfies your needs. But in two hours' time, you're hungry again. That's Sky Sports to me. The presenters are all very well dressed, very articulate, and make excellent points. The studio set is magnificent. The gadgets are magnificent. The analysis is to the point. They do everything right. But you ask somebody two hours later what was said? Nobody remembers, because it's fast-food analysis.

Say what you like about myself and O'Rourke and Brolly, but whatever we said, people remembered. They remembered that night and they were talking about it still the following day in the shops and the creameries and the schools and the staff rooms. And chances are, still talking about it on Tuesday as well. That's the sign of good analysis: if they're still talking about what you said a couple of days later. But I think that's exactly what *The Sunday Game* forgot, and when I look at the way things are going now I'd ask if we learned our lesson from being obsessed with Sky.

I can remember Declan McBennett giving a presentation when he became Head of Sport in RTÉ, and he gave us a photocopy of what he believed was the best sports analysis programme in the world. It was a photocopy of an article from *The Times* on *Monday Night Football*, with Gary Neville and Jamie Carragher on for three hours. The first hour was a deep-dive analysis of the games of the previous week, then analysis of the game on that night and then back to more analysis of previous games. It's terrific, red-hot in terms of production values and so on, and McBennett was very keen on it – five full minutes on Burnley's zonal marking for corner kicks and so on.

What was interesting to me, though, is that the biggest audience *Monday Night Football* ever had was for a discussion: a debate on the proposed European Super League. It was a passionate debate with plenty of argument involved from Neville and Carragher but there were no gadgets involved and there was no deep-dive analysis. It was just a passionate discussion on a topic both of them felt deeply about.

I think over the years we forgot that that's what we were good at – debate with plenty of back and forth, a bit of humour, a bit of craic. But when I look at rugby analysis now, in particular, I often feel GAA analysis is going the same way. There can be an element of 'If you can't convince, then confuse'. That's particularly true when it comes to the jargon. When I hear the co-commentator or the analysts talking about how this team are playing a low block, or the other crowd are playing a mid-block or a high block, which isn't helping them in transition. Or this forward is trying a back-door cut or a V cut and he's not executing it properly … Without being condescending, does Paddy Murphy in Cahersiveen or Joe Murphy in Inishowen actually know what a low block is? Do 90 per cent of the population know what a V cut is? Do they care? We're reaping what we sow because years ago we installed a lot of bluffers and spoofers as coaches. There are a lot of them now employed in sports analysis and the GAA is no different to any other sports. This is the result.

I had great days with *The Sunday Game*. I didn't fall out with any of the pundits. The only half-dodgy time was the night of an All-Ireland final, because some fellas might, on the way back to the studio, go for a pint or two. We certainly had one night definitely, if not two, when one of our panellists was absolutely full. In fairness, the rest of the lads carried him.

Declan McBennett is in place now, and he's a good guy – strong, independently minded and used to getting his own way. He's big into stats. He lives in south Armagh so would have been conscious of any anti-Ulster bias, real or imagined. He'd also be immersed in social media.

I don't think there is a sports programme anywhere in the world that gets more social media attention than *The Sunday Game*, but the recurring theme on social media for years – before Declan came in – would have been: 'I never watch *The Sunday Game*' or 'When the analysis comes on *The Sunday Game* then I switch over to Sky, the analysis is much better there'. That was a narrative which accompanied Declan when he came in, but it was incorrect. When you looked at the viewing figures on Sky, you realised that it couldn't be correct because their viewing figures were terrible. Clearly there was no one 'leaving' *The Sunday Game* when the analysis started.

But that illustrated the power of social media to influence thinking in RTÉ. A minority of people are on social media, and a minority of those were active about *The Sunday Game*. You could break it down to a tiny percentage of the population and then step back and ask, 'Should 5 per cent of the population be driving the narrative about a programme?' In the last four or five years, I would have challenged that narrative in relation to social media.

I know it was also important to bring in new faces, and it was a new period of inclusivity signalled by bringing in women, and that I can understand. But in the television world, you could argue that the rush to embrace inclusivity helped with the practice of exclusivity, because the older man was pushed out: ageism, in other words.

I respected Declan – what you see is what you get and I didn't have any issue with him, but he said from the outset that one of his aims was to get rid of the celebrity analysts. I remember Michael Lyster advising against that on the basis that Joanne Cantwell was new as a presenter and it wouldn't be fair to surround her with inexperienced analysts. She needed a bedding-in period and a few experienced panellists would help.

You look back now and ask if the likes of Eamon Dunphy and George Hook were bad pundits? I don't think so. I think they and the GAA lads generated huge interest and brought in big audiences. The irony now is that when you look at Sky, the channel that set the standard, they seem to be going back to the older pundit, for want of a better word. Graeme Souness and Roy Keane – those are the pundits Sky use now, which is pursuing the RTÉ course.

Declan was very much hands-on, more of a micromanager than some of his predecessors. Some of the Heads of Sport you'd hardly see from one end of the year to the other, unless you were dealing with a contract, but not Declan. The first year in the job he brought half the analysts together for a meeting in Dublin, and the other half in Cork. On those occasions, he gave us a bit of a pep talk, a little bit like a school principal talking to students.

Did he ever say what he wanted us to talk about or avoid talking about? Did he ever tell us what to do? No. The only point he made was that no matter what we said – someone should be sacked or someone should have got a red card – as long as we could back that point up with evidence, then he had no problem.

* * *

I suspected that I'd be one of the first 'celebrity panellists' out the door when Declan landed in. He rang me up for a general chat, but I could tell from the gist of the conversation what was up. He spoke a lot about Stephen Cluxton calling it a day and knowing it was time to call it a day, which was a fairly clear signal to me on the other end of the line (though Cluxton is still trucking, of course). I was pleading with him to hold on, I was making my case, but he said he was coming down to meet me in Killarney. I knew well what was coming.

As it happened, a relation of mine died suddenly in tragic circumstances the day before we were supposed to meet, so we cancelled that meeting. Then we were supposed to meet for coffee and something else came up, so between one thing and another we managed to kick the can down the road.

I got to work as far into the championship as the All-Ireland semi-final, then the final, so I was just about holding on. Then Joe got the bullet, and I got another couple of years out of it.

To be fair to Declan, he was aware that I wanted to hold on because I was under financial pressure. As I'll explain later, my experiences with CEDRA (the Commission for the Economic Development of Rural Areas) and rural Ireland meant I took a financial hit, and Declan gave me a break, which was a big help to me at that point. I'd certainly be grateful for that.

I would disagree with some of his approach. He probably came in with too many pre-set ideas rather than sussing out the lie of the land, and he maybe wanted to be in control of everything. Is that a failing? Maybe, but having said that, he never interfered directly with us either. We had our own statistics team on the programme, and we knew he was big into deep-dive analysis and liked his statistics. For about a year and a half, as a result, I became obsessed with them. I was hoping I could keep Declan happy and maybe I'd get another year on the programme.

Then, having survived that year, he asked to meet me in Cork, and I thought I was definitely getting the bullet at that sit-down, but I didn't. He gave me a two-year contract, but added that that would be my last one. That was disappointing, but on the other hand, because I knew I had just the two years left, I felt liberated when it came to analysis. My attitude was 'Feck it, I'm not going to be here for much longer, so I don't have to think in terms of the next round of contract negotiations'.

Instead of being obsessed with stats, I felt free. I've referred to the number of bluffers and spoofers at large in Gaelic games, the lads throwing out the low block and the high block. I specifically remember one time being told by a person that I should bear in mind that football has changed since I played, that I was 67 and the game was very different to when I played. That's rubbish. The ball is still the same. The team that scores more than the opposition still wins the game. The tactics have changed, of course, but the principles haven't. And I then felt free to analyse in my own style once again.

I gave a talk at a coaching course a couple of years ago and I recognised the look on some of the faces in the audience – they're looking up at this dinosaur talking away on the stage. I said to myself, 'I'm going to leave an impression on these boys today, and I'm going to give them something different.'

Before arriving for the course I'd had a look on Google for a sport whose drills would be applicable in Gaelic football, and I came up with Olympic handball. Advanced hand-passing drills and so on? Ideal. A friend of mine put them on slides so I could use them in a PowerPoint presentation, and I used that at the coaching course.

I said, 'Lads, have a look at these drills.' I could see the impression they left on the coaches in the audience. These were innovative drills they'd never seen before and they were obviously bursting to get back to their teams to use them in training. For a minute or two I was tempted to chance my arm and take the credit for reinventing the wheel, but my conscience got the better of me.

'Lads, I'm only bluffing it because I just pulled this stuff in from Olympic handball.'

The difference is I owned up to it. How many of the bluffers at large in Gaelic games ever do that?

I decided to be myself those last two years and to park the deep-dive analysis, and I was a lot better in terms of analysis as a result.

There were other challenges. We had to deal with Covid, which was no joke. You'd leave home and you mightn't eat again for the rest of the day. There were highlights like good games and wins for Kerry, but the stand-out was the commemoration of Bloody Sunday in Croke Park. That was a special occasion. When the lights were turned down and the flames shone on Hill 16 and Brendan Gleeson gave his oration, the list of names of people killed … I thought it was spine-tingling, and I felt privileged to be in the stadium for it. It was magical.

When I came to 2022, though, I was getting enough of it. For one, the driving was beginning to lose its appeal. I'm 67 and getting into the car in Ballybofey for a seven-hour spin home wasn't that attractive anymore. In 2022, I covered a game in Castlebar, and after the final whistle I got back to the car pretty quickly but the car never moved for 40 minutes. An hour and a quarter later I was at the outskirts of Castlebar. Not fun.

Take a National League Sunday. For one thing, it's not a Sunday, it's a weekend. There might be three games on the Saturday to cover to get the gist of what happened and have your analysis prepared. Then you'd leave home at half seven on a Sunday morning to head to RTÉ and only get out of the studio at half eleven the same night to arrive back home at four o'clock or later. I did that a lot of the time. Sometimes, you could stay in a hotel, but if you did you'd hardly sleep because you were getting in so late after the programme, your mind would still be racing. So, the long haul back home was taxing.

When you're beginning to get weary of that, smaller things begin to grate more. For instance, the greatest pricks in the business are the fellas who are given a hi-vis jacket to act as parking stewards; Our Lord himself wouldn't get a space near the ground with those lads on duty.

On top of all of that, towards the end, social media was starting to get stuck into us. It wasn't taking over my life but it was becoming an itch, put it that way. Instead of dealing with whatever point I had made, I was getting plenty of personal attacks: I was too old, out of touch, this and that. If the focus was on my comments on a game I wouldn't have minded.

Then the focus switched to one of my family members. I didn't expect that. It was an incorrect statement about a member of my family, and that statement drew more reactions, all expanding on the original falsehood. I don't want to relive that time by repeating the lie, but I couldn't let it slide. I wasn't happy at all. My daughter would be good when it comes to using social media and so on, so when I told her I wanted this false narrative corrected, she got to work. She set up an anonymous account and used that to contact those in charge of the site. She pointed out that the site was publishing false allegations which needed to be removed. And in fairness, they did.

But by then I had a bee in my bonnet. I studied a few of the posts from the person who had first come out with the falsehood and a couple of things struck me.

'Do you know something,' I said to my daughter, 'I think

this fella is from around home, based on a couple of these comments.'

She went through all this person's posts and picked out a dozen that gave away certain hints about their location. After reading seven of them, I could identify exactly who it was and that he was someone I knew. After the 2022 All-Ireland final Kerry won, of course, he was one of the thousands of fellas I met.

I knew what I felt like saying to him that day, but I didn't bother. I had already made it known to people in the area that I knew who was posting falsehoods online about my family.

＊ ＊ ＊

I was getting tired in 2022. I was 32 years on the road, but I still felt that I was justifying my presence on the show because I was still getting a reaction, it was still relevant.

The first game of the year I covered was Mayo v Galway, and at half-time, I made a mistake. I very rarely made mistakes, but on this occasion, I got the name of the goalscorer wrong. The same day, the sun was hitting the monitor at an angle and I couldn't see it that clearly. As a result, I made that mistake at half-time during the analysis.

Declan texted Rory O'Neill, the producer, and Joanne Cantwell to say that after the break I had to apologise for the mistake, but neither of them told me. The next morning, I had an email from Declan's secretary, saying he wanted to meet me in his office the following Wednesday at two o'clock.

I rang Rory O'Neill, and he said the message had come in during the game but they didn't bother telling me. If they had, I'd have acknowledged the mistake, absolutely

I was going to Portugal for a wedding, so I couldn't meet Declan that day, so another meeting was arranged for the following week. I was saying to myself, 'I'm 67 years of age in December but I'm supposed to leave home at 6.30 a.m. to drive to Dublin, probably to be told this was my last year on the programme.'

But when I came back from Portugal, a new contract came in the door for the programme – one which would have put me on a salary not far away from what I was getting 30 years prior. No one in RTÉ at that time realised I was already on a contract, though we've all found out since that keeping track of contracts isn't really RTÉ's forte. That contract came in eight weeks in a row, at 9.50 every Friday morning, but I was thinking, 'Do I really need this, to go up and meet Declan about this?' I eventually realised that it was the push I needed to go.

Everything I've done in life, in teaching or in football, I've left of my own accord. Thirty years was a good run. I left with no regrets and no bitterness towards anyone. It was only when I announced my retirement that I realised I should have done so 20 years earlier, because everyone was nice to me suddenly.

The good wishes, the mass cards, the vouchers – the goodwill was unbelievable. I had a great innings with *The Sunday Game*; I was privileged to be allowed into people's living rooms for 30 years. I was relevant to them. They spoke about me, they liked me, and 95 per cent of them were positive. No regrets.

CHAPTER 16

REALITY AND RURAL IRELAND

For much of my time on *The Sunday Game*, I was also running the family bar, but there were big differences between my time and my mother's day. And some of those differences illustrate perfectly the changes in rural Ireland that I've seen in my time.

For instance, there were no performing rights payments in the early days. When I took over it was different because rural bars weren't treated differently compared to city bars when it came to something like performing rights.

What did I have in the bar? A radio that didn't sound great in the background and a television that was switched on for matches. But that didn't matter, because under performing rights legislation, I had to pay a fee and the fee was based on my floor area. I could have the same floor area, or bigger, than a pub in Temple Bar, so I had to pay more money than them because of the floor area.

Another difference is that, in my mother's time, cash was king. Literally. She kept all her money at home in a black purse she kept in the wardrobe, under the clothes and next to the heater. I always remember that because when we were off on tour for weeks in Australia in 1981, a local woman, Kathleen Moriarty, was brought in to live with my mother while the three of us were away. During that time, the pub was robbed. In fairness, Kathleen didn't tell us about the robbery until we came back because she didn't want to spoil our holiday. When we did get back, we wanted to know if everyone was okay, but we also wanted to know if the thieves got the black purse. They didn't.

I remember a few people that time saying, 'Oh, they wouldn't have robbed the place if you were there,' but, sad to report, they did rob the place two years later and I slept through it. Like a log. That second time, my mother and I were both there, and the robber – or robbers – were so cool about the job that they had time to have two pint-bottles of beer in addition to stealing the cigarettes. Not that they were ever caught after.

* * *

It's one of the things I've always said: with this rural–urban divide, an awful lot of the legislation is urban-led, not rural-based. A case in point? Drink driving. In my mother's day – and when I was there as well, particularly early on – we would have had seven to ten bachelor farmers that came to us four or five nights a week. Three or four cars coming from over the road or down from the hills.

But then when the drink-driving legislation came in – and it wasn't all that strict at first – it had a huge effect. The old people were and are very respectful of the law, which was part of their upbringing, and what happened was they stopped drinking at all if they had to drive.

Now, what did they have? They used to have two or three pints, maybe four. They drove down, they drove up, five nights a week. Did they ever crash, did they ever cause trouble, were they drunk? No. This was their lifeline. This was their outlet in life. When that legislation came in, though, they never came out again.

We didn't have – and we don't have – a bus route. There were two taxis in Kenmare and neither of them was going to drive eight miles out the road to bring a man four miles up a mountain.

Those people never came out again and many of them were dead in a short period of time through loneliness, through isolation, and possibly through suicide in some cases. I don't condone drink driving. Of course not, but if you bring in legislation, you must make sure there's a facility to help people like that.

In my mother's day, and the early days I was there, the bar was the community centre. On a Sunday night in the summer, when the father and mother brought down the kids, they played pool and had a sing-song. Those were the best of times. You'd be putting them out of the bar at about 10.30 and it was still bright.

Then there was a ban on having children in the bar. I could understand the theory behind it, but in a rural area, the bar was the community centre. That destroyed the fabric of the community and was just wrong. Where did the kids go? At least in the bar they were supervised.

In previous years, the publican was a counsellor, a psychologist, an agony aunt. My mother was that for years, and I was that myself. As soon as I could walk, I was behind the counter collecting glasses, so I spent 50 years of my life behind the bar. Twenty-five years working with my mother and the other 25 working for myself.

My mother would have said it – the busy nights were great in the bar when it was buzzing. When there was a sing-song, or when Johnny Bán and Donal Murt would recite the poems of Robert Service. Brilliant.

But on winter nights it could be brutal, with only one or two customers. We had a long bar, so there could be three customers, one on a corner, one in the middle, one in the back, the three of them probably not talking to each other.

I often spent three or four hours down in the bar with some drunk talking away, and you had to tolerate it. I picked up valuable lessons there, though. One was that working behind the bar is a lesson in life because you get to know people. You get to judge people well. I'd be very good at looking at people at a distance and knowing whether they're happy, angry, whether they have a problem with me.

The other thing was *The Sunday Game*. It introduced a different type of clientele – they'd come in with a preconceived notion that they hate you and your antics.

But I was a good barman, fast, and I was good with people. And when you know somebody doesn't like you and they're about to say so, you can say something or crack even half a joke, and suddenly he starts to turn back and realise 'Jesus, he's not as much of a bollocks as I thought'. And then you try another joke, and you have them cracked.

Our big customers came from the North, particularly when the three of us were still playing with Kerry. From the 12th of July to the middle of August, they were here. They were GAA fanatics, they drank for Ireland, they spent for Ireland and they did a tour of the Kerry spots. That was their pilgrimage. They'd hit Tim Kennelly's place in Listowel, Páidí Ó Sé's back in Ventry, down to Mick O'Dwyer in Waterville, and then they'd land in to us around three o'clock and we'd get two hours' great spending out of them. But again, when drink driving came in, that business was gone.

The other great lesson from the bar business, outside of knowing people, was realising that some drunk fella abusing you at night might call the following day and apologise: 'Yes, I'm really sorry about that. I was drunk last night and shouldn't have said all of that, I was out of order.'

But the one thing I can truly say is *in vino veritas* – with wine comes the truth. The drunken fella who's abusing you is telling you exactly what he wants to tell you. I know that for a fact, and I will never ever accept the 'No, I didn't mean that'. A drunken person speaks with a sober mind. No doubt about it.

* * *

I spent 50 years behind the bar counter. I spent 35 years as a teacher. In both jobs, you're a performer. You're an actor. Behind the counter is your stage. Standing in front of the blackboard is your stage.

And when you have a stage, you have to be nice. It didn't matter whether you felt half-drunk or hungover going to school in the morning; you couldn't appear drunk or hungover, you had to be bright and happy. The same with the bar, it didn't matter if you were grumpy, cranky or felt the whole world was against you. Once you went inside the counter, you had to be happy and bright to customers.

In a bar, every customer had to be treated with respect. My mother's view was that the customer is always right and I carried that through with me too; we were always good to customers. We were kind to customers and considerate to people. We dealt with long-standing issues: the fella on his own, drunk, could be spilling out his troubles with me for two or three hours, and if he wanted help I'd maybe meet him again and do whatever I could.

After we got married, Rosarii was pregnant with one of the kids and I was doing *The Sunday Game*. I was coming down after one of the programmes and a customer rang Rosarii on the house phone – no mobiles at the time – to say that he had a gun and he was going to commit suicide. This was a good friend of ours. Rosarii didn't know what to do, but she got another customer in the bar to drive up to your man's house and see what was going on, to bring him down to the bar. She rang him back and said the customer was going up to collect him, to come down for a chat.

I came home from Dublin, and myself and Rosarii and this man sat in the kitchen the entire night. We talked through everything and listened to him. We rang his father the following day to collect him, and he's perfect since – he never looked back.

Rosarii went into labour prematurely a couple of weeks later, and I would imagine it was partly because of that night. That's an extreme instance but a good example of how we helped people out over the years.

* * *

In terms of my own attitude to or relationship with drink, I enjoy a drink myself. Would I abuse it? I don't think I would. Can I take my drink? Unfortunately, I can.

We had some customers whose capacity to drink was unreal. I don't want to be flippant, but a fella said to me once, 'It isn't a thirst I have, it's a gift,' and he wasn't wrong. I remember one of our best customers, and his ambition for the day of his 40th birthday was to drink 40 pints, and in the course of the day he went to about 30 pints.

I see the issues of alcoholism all over, and the one thing that we were always trying to be in the bar was responsible. We didn't do after-hours, and by not doing so, or by refusing a drink to somebody who's already drunk, you could be the worst in the world and you'd get cursed out of it. But you also know if you refuse someone, it's different to a city bar, because if you refuse someone and he gets the hump and walks out, he could be taking one-third of your customers with him when family and neighbours get involved.

I gave my time driving fellas home drunk, but there were plenty of fellas who wouldn't listen to reason as well, fellas that fucked me out of it and wouldn't get out of the car even though they were in no shape to drive.

The big change for us was that we were a country bar four miles from Kenmare and 13, 14 miles from Sneem. We had a good bar but, in real terms, three months' trade had to equal what we'd take the other nine months of the year. June, July and August equalled the other nine months. We had about six customers those other nine months, and by customer I mean a fellow who drinks, say, four nights a week. We had about six customers within a three-mile radius. It wasn't the case that the rest of the people within three miles of the bar were going somewhere else – they weren't going anywhere at all. So, we were trying to make a living with six customers.

There were other complications. There was a fella I crossed swords with on a football field – we had words and I fucked him out of it or whatever, which wouldn't be unusual for me, certainly. After that incident, though, for four Friday nights in a row there was a garda checkpoint near my bar that eventually nailed three of my customers. That reduced my business by 30 to 40 per cent.

I remember complaining to the gardaí that I was being targeted here, that this was a personal thing. The answer I got was that when the gardaí in question left Tralee on duty, it was a lottery as to where they'd end up. I said you could hardly leave Tralee and end up 200 yards from Pat Spillane's bar four Fridays in a row and describe it as a lottery with a straight face.

What stood to us, though, was that we never did after-hours, even on New Year's Eve. Our tradition was that on New Year's Eve the last half-hour all the drinks were free, which not many places would do.

But one night that rule was broken. I had a very, very prominent politician in the bar – he had three friends with him, and then there was me, serving. It was 12.30 at night and the squad car pulled into the yard behind the bar.

It was able to drive up to the window and the gardaí could see into the bar where I was sitting having a pint with the politician and his friends. We were sitting there for what seemed like an age but was maybe minutes in reality, and I cracked: 'Look, I better go out to them.'

I went out and said, 'So and so is inside,' hoping that the garda would recognise the sensitivity of the situation.

'I don't give a fuck who's inside,' said the garda. 'He has to go.'

Doomsday.

I went in and told them: 'Lads, ye have to go.' And the politician said to fill three more pints.

The guards are in the car at the window. The three lads are at the counter.

What do you do?

I filled the three pints and we sat down. High Noon stuff. The sweat was prickling my forehead.

Again, it seemed like hours, but after a minute or two the guards drove off.

'What did I tell you?' said the politician, lifting his pint.

That wasn't my only encounter with bureaucracy over the years, of course. But my experiences later, after chairing CEDRA and becoming a rural ambassador, showed me just how much bureaucracy can punish the ordinary citizen.

CHAPTER 17

UNDER THE MICROSCOPE

I'm 67 now and I've had a great life. Thirty years on *The Sunday Game*, almost 40 years as a publican, 30 years plus as a teacher, 30 years with the *Sunday World* – I've loved life and I've lived life, and I look back at all of those days with happy memories. When I retired, I wanted to do something to give back to the country I loved and the people of rural Ireland. But my only regret is getting involved with the government to try to help solve the problems of rural Ireland.

* * *

I began to pick up on the struggle. The struggle to field underage teams. The struggles of dying towns. Garda stations closing. Pubs closing. Fellas going away. Reforestation, which to me always means the end of a farm and the end of the family that farmed there if forests are being reintroduced.

I went to a meeting in Kenmare one day and I was disillusioned because there was no plan. Similar meetings were full of negativity, or politicians telling you how much good they were doing. You ended up saying to yourself, 'If you were really doing that well, we wouldn't be here.' State agencies were providing stats to show how well things were going, but I was wondering if that's the case why are there 100 people in the hall looking for change?

At the time, Phil Hogan was the minister responsible for rural Ireland, and whatever contact I had, I got on to him. He asked me would I chair CEDRA (Committee for the Economic Development of Rural Areas)?

For context, this was 2012 and the country was still finding its way through the effects of the economic crash. I was worried rural Ireland was being left behind. I accepted the job. I thought it was a chance to transform rural Ireland. I was going to be the caped crusader and was going to solve everything, but after the first CEDRA meeting, I was so deflated it was unreal.

I went back to the minister and said, 'Look, I come from a sporting background, and in a sporting context, if everyone is wearing a green and gold jersey then they're playing for my county and they're with me. If they're in blue and white they're with my club and they're with me. But I was just at a meeting and there was *no one* with me.'

Hogan was a sharp guy: 'Pat, they're Gaelic full-backs – they're only there to protect their own area. They're literally minding the square, which is their own little patch.'

That's the rock I perished on, and it's the rock that rural Ireland is still perishing on, because we haven't a plan for rural Ireland. We have lots of great people working in rural Ireland, and lots of great ideas. We have hundreds of organisations purporting to be working on various issues in rural Ireland but all of them are operating in parallel universes. There is no joined-up thinking.

When I arrived, I was upsetting the gravy train. Each agency's little patch was under threat. The annual grant could be in danger. That was my first mistake.

When I was appointed chair of CEDRA I got a phone call from someone in the minister's office saying a prominent journalist would ring me for a puff piece. I was surprised – and a little flattered – that a prominent journalist would do such a piece on me, but looking back now I should have realised how those relationships exist between politicians and media – you scratch my back and I scratch yours. Journalists being used by politicians, being fed stories. I should have understood that better but I admit I was full of romantic notions of what we might achieve.

When we got up and running, we travelled all over to meetings to come up with a jobs plan for rural Ireland. At the meetings we met great people. One wet night in Scarriff in Clare, in the community centre there were 150 people spread out in different rooms to come up with plans. Ballingarry in Limerick was another great experience.

Then there was Mayo. What a county. If only we had the entrepreneurial spirit of Mayo nationwide. You see it in McHale Farm Machinery, Smyths Toys, the Hughes brothers with Portwest – brilliant people, great meetings.

I can recall going up a narrow road outside Balla in Mayo to Monaghan Brothers, fitted kitchens and bars. Their customers were the top hotels and bars in Dublin, all being supplied by this unit 140 miles away – a brilliant business.

Donal Byrne's Big Red Barn in Swinford was another classic example. He was making modular homes – ten years ago, don't forget – and I was thinking he could help solve the homelessness problem overnight. But he told me about dealing with government departments, dealing with the red tape and bureaucracy.

No surprise there. I've often said about Ireland that if there was an Olympic competition for bureaucracy and red tape, Ireland would be the gold-medal winners every time.

Another traditional challenge for rural Ireland is access to finance. Good broadband? Another headache. But bureaucracy is a real killer. Byrne was banging his head off a brick wall with the various agencies. He ended up selling far more modular homes to Sierra Leone than to Ireland at that time.

These are the great people that are out there, but there are so many barriers in front of them it's unbelievable. They should be looking at stepping stones, not stumbling blocks.

When we were tasked with coming up with a jobs plan, there were three points to consider. What are the job opportunities in this rural area? How best can these job opportunities be realised? And what are the challenges?

The first meeting started with the last one, challenges, and that destroyed the meeting immediately; challenges led to negativity, and negativity killed the meeting.

After that, we started with the other points – the job opportunities in this area and how best to realise them. We started with positivity and that meant we got great ideas. There wasn't a night we got to the negativity of the challenges.

But at every night and at every meeting, we were marked by whatever quango or organisation was on hand. The farmers were brilliant at that: it didn't matter where we were, there were three or four farmers' representatives present. They had their script, they had their mantra and the prepared points were delivered to perfection.

I say they were brilliant because they were worried about farming, that maybe grants could be affected. One of my first meetings in the job was with the IFA (Irish Farmers' Association), and I thought this was great, we'd work together. In fairness to the guy from the IFA, when we met I was saying about our plans that we'd work on this together, a rising tide lifts all boats, if something good is happening inside the farm gate, it'll have a good impact outside the farm gate …

He looked me in the eye and said, 'Pat, can I tell you something? We're a lobby group for farmers. We don't give a fuck what happens outside the farm gate.'

He was honest and that gave me clarity. They are a lobby group and they bat hard for the farmers.

* * *

We still came up with great ideas, and our plan is still the plan for rural Ireland. Our ideas are still the ideas to be implemented. But the issue with quangos minding their own corner remains.

When CEDRA was set up by Hogan, it had to be co-sponsored by another government department, so it was the Department of the Environment and the Department of Agriculture together. This was a problem, because it meant going back to definitions – how you defined rural Ireland. And this was where agriculture came in because, in the farmers' eyes, farming is rural Ireland. But the reality is that the majority of people that live in rural Ireland don't live on farms. They live outside the farm gate: rural Ireland is no longer farming.

In addition, the Department of Agriculture, our co-sponsors, viewed us with suspicion. For the public meetings, especially the big meetings, the Department of Agriculture never came to any of them. Never. At all the public meetings all over Ireland, was there ever anyone from the Department of Agriculture to say any proposal was a good idea? Not a bit of it.

Of course, because there's a big bundle of money coming from the government and from Europe, the farming sector was going to hang onto that bundle of money, no matter what.

Because of that, the CEDRA stakeholder meetings themselves could be soul-destroying. The first couple of meetings had academics arguing about the definition of rural Ireland: I couldn't handle that at all. Any definition of rural Ireland aired at those CEDRA meetings that referred to inside the farm gate, and the Department of Agriculture representative atthese meetings, which they did attend, who wouldn't have spoken before and wouldn't speak afterwards, would pipe up with one of three stock responses.

It was either, 'Excuse me, Mr Chairman, this is not within your terms of reference.'

Right, slap on wrist.

Or it could be, 'Excuse me, Mr Chairman, this is not within your remit.'

Slap on wrist.

Or – and this came from an older guy who was at one of the meetings – it could be, 'Excuse me, Mr Chairman, this subject matter is *ultra vires*.'

Slap.

It was absolutely soul-destroying. You can talk about the good news stories in rural Ireland, but there are a lot of bad news stories as well. And until such time as the stakeholders work together with a targeted plan, that will continue.

When it came time for our big report to be compiled, Cathal O'Donoghue, a great man from Teagasc, was a huge help. The two of us were summoned by the Department of Agriculture to an early-morning meeting to outline the main points of the report in advance.

There were four or five there to meet us, including Simon Coveney, then the minister. (In my memory, they were sitting at a table on a slightly higher level than ours for some reason.) Coveney was well briefed, to be fair, but after a few minutes, the meeting changed. Once the officials realised that we weren't looking for anything out of the farm budget for CEDRA, they switched off. It was clear they didn't care anymore. They didn't give a shit, and I can prove that by the level of interest they had in the report, even though they were officially its co-authors.

When the day came for the report itself to be published, several media outlets contacted the Department of

Agriculture for copies, but there wasn't a copy of the report in the department. An urgent phone call was made to Teagasc in Athenry where Cathal O'Donoghue had to load a bunch of reports into the boot of his car and drive them to Dublin. That is how invested in rural Ireland the department was.

* * *

No matter how you define rural Ireland, the easiest way to identify the parts which are struggling is to look at the rural GAA club. That's the barometer. You can look at unemployment and poverty indices, and depopulation, but if the GAA club is doing well, with good numbers in all the age groups, then the area is probably okay.

But if the club is struggling to field teams ... all along the western seaboard, clubs amalgamate to field underage teams, and that's always a giveaway about the hinterland those clubs are drawing from. The facts back me up.

About ten years ago, a survey in Kerry showed there were 76 GAA clubs in the county but about one-third of them were drawing from areas which had fewer than eight boys per class in their national school. Eight clubs had fewer than five boys per class.

In some south Kerry clubs, it was even worse. Derrynane had fewer than three boys per class, Skellig Rangers and Portmagee had fewer than four per class.

Asdee in north Kerry? Two or fewer. Valentia, Renard, Dromid – much the same.

The figures are probably worse now, but ten years ago two-thirds of all clubs couldn't field fifteen U17 players. At the time of the survey, in the 16 to 21 age group in school, Derrynane had three registered players: three. Tuosist had eight. Asdee had ten.

That's the barometer. If an area has two boys per class, or four boys, then you know there's trouble ahead.

Some busy towns and villages have hidden problems. Dingle is a lively spot and a fine town, but the GAA club has to amalgamate to field teams. It doesn't have kids.

Population numbers can be deceptive and Templenoe is a good example. Around here, there are a lot of holiday homes and a lot of people who've retired. That's fine, but holiday homes have the lights out all winter, and a lot of the people who are retired don't integrate into communities – they keep to themselves. So, you need to target the Templenoes in a different way.

Why? Because so many of the houses and premises are Airbnbs or businesses, there's no room for families. That means fewer kids in the GAA club.

Services for communities and families in rural areas must return. Rural crime is now on the increase, but we closed all the garda stations. In the sixties, we closed the railway lines, which was one of the most moronic decisions ever – closing the railway to Cahersiveen and

Kenmare and Bantry and other places. What a stupid idea that was.

Closing the national schools we had here in the sixties was also stupid, because we had a population to sustain them. We need a targeted plan for those peripheral areas or those towns and villages that are struggling.

* * *

Other factors didn't help our cause. For instance, there's a little bit of rural in every department: transport, environment, health. But no one takes overall responsibility. Rural Ireland no longer has a department devoted to it, it's been folded into the Department of Social Protection instead. That means a small budget, which in turn forces the civil servants into *The Late Late Show* approach: one for everyone in the audience. Small grants for this local group, for that greenway plan, enough for them to keep ticking over without ever working to a national coordinated plan.

The absence of a national body doesn't help either. The Dairy Council is in charge of dairy matters; An Bord Bia is in charge of food. Those are clearly defined responsibilities. There's none of that for rural Ireland.

We dealt with Údarás na Gaeltachta in CEDRA, and they're very good because they're focused on a particular area: the economic and social development of the Gaeltacht areas. We need something similar to look after rural Ireland.

Policy in Ireland is created by the central government, but it's the people on the ground who have the answers. CEDRA was about a bottom-up approach where you went to the people on the ground and they came up with the answers which fed into the plan.

On the other hand, some public servants are brilliant policy-makers, but in many cases, they're civil servants living in Dublin, not rural areas. They live in Leopardstown or Fairview and come into work on the Luas to an office near Trinity College; they don't have a feel for rural Ireland. Whatever about other areas of policy, this background will not give you insight into rural Ireland; hence the east-coast solutions to west-coast problems.

There were dangers in crossing some of those civil servants, too. After one meeting in the department, I remember a very nice lady saying to me, 'You know, you're not going to win the war with these people. My advice to you is choose a battle and try to win that battle, because you're not going to win the war.' She was spot on, because if you decide to go to war with the permanent government and the various departments, you are seriously up against it.

* * *

One of the great rural TDs was the late Paddy Sheehan from West Cork. When talking about the Mizen peninsula years ago, he said if nothing was done for Mizen, all that would be left there would be briars, bachelors and bullocks. On my travels I saw a lot of places that fit that description.

That's why positivity was a big driving force for me at the meetings. At every one of them, I tried to deliver two messages about why we could succeed. One was Micko's message about believing in yourself, which he drove into us for years. The second came from Jimmy McGuinness. He took over Donegal when they were ranked 19th in Ireland and the mantra they repeated in the dressing-room before every training session and game was: commit, focus, believe, achieve. You can adopt that mantra to any task.

A good example of how to achieve came just a couple of years ago, when we saw one stubborn narrative utterly demolished. That was the long-standing belief that young people didn't want to live in rural Ireland, just like big companies didn't want to set up in rural Ireland because they needed airports for connectivity. This was a long-standing IDA belief. There's a reason I haven't even mentioned the IDA yet in this context; they're a joke. They've done nothing for rural counties or peripheral areas.

Where our state agencies fell down was in not selling other aspects of rural Ireland. Forget what we don't have. What *do* we have? Quality of life. Empty roads. Loads of houses, or we had at one time. Places in the school for your kids.

We were told young people didn't want to live in rural Ireland, but we accidentally found out the truth with Covid. That brought the youngsters back home, and guess what? They discovered that they could work from home. They had a great quality of life, and rural Ireland was affordable. There was as much craic over a weekend around Kenmare, or their nearest town, as you'd have over a weekend in Dublin. We still haven't capitalised on that enough, but at least it buried one lazy myth.

* * *

We got the CEDRA report out after a year and a half of hard work travelling the country. It was launched in February 2013 by Enda Kenny – a great man, an honourable man and a rural man himself, from Islandeady outside Castlebar. He wanted this plan delivered.

We had a big gathering of politicians and all the various quangos at the Irish Museum of Country Living outside Castlebar for the launch. The speech Kenny gave was brilliant, but there were two disappointments.

I think the *Irish Times* might have been the only print media in attendance; there was no real mention of the launch elsewhere. That's because – and you couldn't make this up – at the very time Enda Kenny was delivering his address, Pat McGrath of RTÉ was outside the venue interviewing Phil Hogan live for the one o'clock news.

Was he expanding on this good news story? No, Phil was denying the latest scare story about the new water charges. So, instead of having a good news story about rural Ireland, the report was lost amid the firefighting about Irish Water, and got little traction. An omen.

When Phil Hogan left the Department of the Environment, the lead department driving CEDRA, Alan Kelly took over and a junior minister, Ann Phelan, came in to look after CEDRA.

Alan's a good friend of mine and a passionate politician, but unfortunately he was handed the water charges, and rural Ireland went to the back of the queue. To be fair, he set up an advisory body to drive job creation in rural Ireland, but all the usual people from all the usual quangos were there. People who never created a job in their lives but were somehow supposed to know how to create jobs. I'd seen them already at meetings, busy on their laptops until something threatened their organisation's budget.

I said we should have an advisory committee with entrepreneurs, businesspeople: fellas who had created jobs. I got people like Pat McDonagh, who started with one chip shop and now has Supermac's outlets all over the country. I got Edmund Harty from north Kerry, who took over his father's Dairymaster milking-machine company in Causeway and made it one of the top milking-machine producers in Europe. A brilliant guy. The third man was Chris Martin, an Englishman and head of Musgrave's.

Another great addition. What we learned from these lads' expertise was off the charts.

Unfortunately, we stayed at the back of the queue because the minister was bogged down with water charges.

When Heather Humphries came in as minister for rural development, I was appointed ambassador for the rural action plan. Michael Ring was the junior minister – a passionate rural man, I will say that.

In the intervening period, an action plan for jobs in rural Ireland was published, involving all departments and with targets for all departments. Humphreys and Ring set up a monitoring committee – in theory, a great idea, as it had representatives from every department and from the rural stakeholders.

The problem was that these were stakeholders as determined by a computer – the usual suspects, in other words. At our first meeting in Athlone, those stakeholders sat on one side of the room and the departmental representatives sat across on the other side. I spoke at the meeting and said this wasn't good for the optics – us versus them. We had to work together.

Another mistake. Another target on my back.

The monitoring committee was a joke. Instead of challenging departments about their targets, the meetings had presentations by quangos proclaiming how good they were. Was there any challenge to the targets? No. And the officials understood quickly there was no threat in this monitoring committee. By the third or fourth meeting, the only representative turning up was from the rural department itself. I suggested ESRI economists – independent people – should have been challenging these departments, but that idea went nowhere and eventually the monitoring committee fizzled out.

My job as ambassador was to go around Ireland and see what was working and what wasn't. It was brilliant. Every five or six weeks, I'd go back to tell the minister and officials, 'This is good, this is working, this isn't, it needs some work.'

The rural groups loved me because they thought I was the conduit between them and the department, bringing their stories to Dublin. I was meeting people who were at the coalface: there was real value in their contributions.

The first year was really good. I got on great with the people I was reporting to in Dublin, but at the end of that year, there was no rush to reappoint me for a second year. After a couple of months, I was brought to Dublin for a meeting and told I was being reappointed but for half the fee I got the first year. I was so happy in the job that the money didn't really matter to me. I loved the job. Come year three, I wasn't reappointed – I got a letter thanking me for my work and that was that. I was really upset. There was no falling-out, no dispute.

The following week, *The Late Late Show* asked me to go on, and I said I would. I was really angry, as being dismissed felt like being dropped after scoring five points a game the preceding year. If I had done something wrong, I could have understood, but there was no sense of any tension, apart from the very last meeting I'd had with Michael Ring. That meeting took place before Christmas and I'd come up from a great meeting with a group in Lady's Island in Wexford. I stayed up until 3 a.m. writing my notes. I was buzzing.

The next day, Ring met me with his advisor. I presented what I'd found in Wexford, but I was told that that information needed to be on file. I should have known then that this could be their opportunity to get rid of me because they needed something on file and the material hadn't been typed up.

I was so dumbstruck that I forgot to point out the reason there was nothing on file. According to my contract, which presumably neither of them had read, secretarial assistance was to be provided by the department. I don't type, but every two months or so I'd attend the department and meet the minister. The officials would take my handwritten notes and type them up, and often photocopied them as well. It was their job to do that. Not mine.

Accordingly, when I went on *The Late Late Show* that evening in April, I was critical of the rural Ireland plan and the department, but not so much of the minister himself. I certainly didn't launch any personal attack because he was hard-working and passionate: he reminded me of my neighbours, the Healy-Raes.

That *Late Late Show* was pre-recorded on a Wednesday because the Friday was a Good Friday. We were at home watching on the Friday, and the programme hadn't even finished when the texts started landing on my phone.

The tone was worrying – there was a shot or two across the bows – but I was sitting at home with the family and couldn't tell them what was coming through on my phone. The general gist was that things were going to get tough because I'd upset the firm.

* * *

From then on, there were stories about me in the newspapers on a regular basis.

The Late Late Show aired on 19 April 2019 and two days later the *Sunday Independent* carried a big story featuring copies of text messages I'd sent to Michael Ring, as well as the details of my salary. Shortly afterwards, the *Mayo News* carried more of the same.

There was even more going on behind the scenes. Almost a year after that story broke, in February 2020, the journalist Ken Foxe uncovered some interesting facts about freedom of information requests made by Michael Ring to RTÉ about what I earned with the national broadcaster. I don't know to this day what relevance that had to my work on rural Ireland, but it later emerged that RTÉ had advised him on how to obscure his identity when making those requests. Disappointing, given I worked for RTÉ for 30 years.

This was the drip-drip-drip of public assassination. I was told by some people it was because I was being outspoken. Outspoken? Is that a crime? A minister in a government department wanted to know what I was earning in my private life. I was outspoken and that was the result? I was told I was high-profile and in the limelight – was that making people unhappy?

That April, TD Thomas Byrne tweeted: 'Let me get this straight, a citizen criticises the minister, and the minister demands his employers reveal the citizen's salary and private information. How is this happening? GDPR?'

Also on 21 April 2019, the *Sunday Times* had a headline: 'Minister challenges RTÉ to reveal Pat Spillane's salary'.

The following month the *Sunday Independent* ran another story: 'Spillane sent officials handwritten report'. When the reporter rang me about that one, I remembered to ask where he'd gotten the information to begin with. Through a freedom of information request, he said, and he started reading out material from my file, saying, 'You did a lot of travelling, you worked hard.'

I pointed out his mistake – that the department were to give me secretarial support according to my contract.

'Hang on,' he said, 'I have your contract here in front of me … you're right.'

They still ran the story, of course.

* * *

It took a huge toll on me. I go for a walk in the forests in Templenoe a couple of days a week and every Saturday without fail. For months on end during my Saturday walk I'd be dreading a call from a Dublin number because I'd know if the call came it would be followed by 'We're running a story tomorrow about you ...'

'You're Pat Spillane, you're high profile.' That was the justification.

On a couple of occasions they had to pull the plug because I threatened legal action. The stories they had in mind were absolutely wrong, completely false. I'd ask why they were chasing me, but there was never a clear answer. I felt it had to be an orchestrated campaign but I didn't know who was driving it.

There were plenty of whispering campaigns going on as well – 'Spillane got this, Spillane did that' – which were particularly hard on my family. They were scattered all over Ireland working and hearing their father had done this, that or the other. Rumours and whispers with no substance to them. The plain truth was I'd done nothing outside of a TV interview that was critical of government policy on rural Ireland.

I thought it was never going to stop. To this day when I go for a walk on a Saturday morning and, God forbid, a strange number comes up on my phone, I'm transported back to that time instantly. The feeling isn't pleasant.

It wasn't just the public humiliation in the newspapers, either. It was weeks, months of social media warriors pitching in with their views: brave boys hiding behind a keyboard.

If I thought that was the bad part, how wrong I was. That was just the tip of the iceberg compared to what was coming – the worst two and a half years of my life.

* * *

For that period of time, while there were non-stories popping up regularly about me in the media, I was also being investigated by every possible government department and state agency that could possibly have an interest in me. That's no exaggeration. What my family and I had to endure for those two and a half years was torture.

I'd ask why was I getting so many letters and being called to so many meetings ever since appearing on *The Late Late Show* and the civil servants would always come back with a bland answer: you were just on the file to be investigated or queried. No other explanation.

I found that hard to believe. After appearing on *The Late Late Show* I was summoned to meetings in Limerick, Cork, Tralee, Dublin by every branch of the state you could imagine, and a few you've never heard of.

If readers think I'm overdoing it, consider this scenario. How would you feel if you had two or three civil servants call to your house, sit in the kitchen and interrogate you about aspects of your life? And, while doing so, whisper questions or pass handwritten notes to each other while the interrogation was going on, quizzing you about matters going back 20 years, matters you could barely remember?

That happened to us on a regular basis. Myself and Rosarii found ourselves facing a couple of civil servants for an hour in our own home, being quizzed as though we were criminals. I often wondered how anyone in Ireland got away with any minor breach or bending of the law given how zealous these people were.

Eventually, a day came when one particular inspector came out for some papers, and he told me he was a fellow GAA man. I didn't know him, but he recognised me and said straight out, 'Pat, I don't know why I'm here to investigate you, I've looked at your file and there are no red flags, no reason to investigate.'

I pointed out to all of our official visitors that they only had to look around them at a modest bungalow and two ten-year-old cars in the drive. We weren't living high on the hog. But they quizzed us on everything, asking us to account even for decisions we'd made 20 years before.

Before one meeting I wasn't feeling well and went to the doctor, who was alarmed by my high blood pressure. He said that under no circumstances was I to attend the meeting on account of the stress involved. He provided me with a medical certificate, but when the investigating officials were told that the doctor had instructed me not to attend the meeting on health grounds, and that Rosarii would go instead, I was told the investigation would be 'escalated' to a higher level.

I subsequently attended the meeting, shaking with illness, and was confined to bed for two days afterwards. A medical cert that would be acceptable to a court of law wasn't acceptable to these people.

The meetings were a mixture of interviews, investigations and interrogations. Long periods of silence. Staring. Texting each other. Whispering to each other and prompting questions. Completely intimidating for what were, after all, administrative questions rather than a criminal investigation. When we weren't being visited we were being bombarded by mail. One morning I got up and went to the front door for the post. I found 12 letters from the one government department waiting for me.

Eventually, I had to bring professional advisors with me to some of these meetings, and they were as baffled as me as to these investigations. They'd never seen anything like it. One man with experience of these situations suggested I'd upset powerful people – that that was the only possible explanation.

It went on for two and a half years and was a huge strain, mentally and physically. And financially. I had to take out a credit union loan because earlier decisions on our affairs were reinterpreted years later, at a cost to us. In another case, a government department made a mistake, one which we are still trying to have rectified at the time of writing.

I'd look now at Maurice McCabe and the price he paid for telling the truth about the gardaí, and while I'm not comparing myself to him for an instant, I feel I got the smallest glimpse of what he went through. My admiration for him, and other people like him, knows no bounds.

Our family didn't know what was going on because we didn't tell them. Rosarii knew, obviously, she had to go to some of those meetings with me, but we didn't share that torture with the rest of them.

I doubt I had a full night's sleep for those two and a half years. I was trying to carry on as normal with the analysis on *The Sunday Game*, but panic attacks were a regular occurrence. High blood pressure. Stress. Nightmares. Palpitations.

When I read about the treatment of dissidents in Soviet Russia or Arab countries, I'd be thinking that was almost the same treatment I was getting – but in Ireland. I knew I was being blackguarded, and I was advised to take legal action more than once, but I just wanted to get out the other side rather than heap even more stress on myself and Rosarii.

She was the rock. She knew. The odd night in bed, she'd say to me, 'You're awake, aren't you?' We'd get up and have a cup of tea and she'd calm me down. The question we'd come back to in those hours would be 'Why are they doing this to us?'

I still find it hard to put into words how good she was to me through that time.

* * *

The last investigation eventually concluded. When the letter came in the door to confirm that it was over, myself and Rosarii stood in the kitchen and hugged each other for about 20 minutes. We cried and we comforted each other with the fact that we had our family and we had our health. That was the consolation.

I know I'm not everyone's cup of tea. That I divide opinion. That's based on people's perception of me on TV for a couple of hours a year talking football. It's not based on my real personality or my behaviour in public. I rarely go out socially and I certainly don't try to be the centre of attention when I do. I'm not pontificating in the pub and letting the whole place know what I think at the top of my voice. Most people's opinion of me is based on my view of their county team or favourite player.

But I didn't deserve what happened in those two and a half years. I wouldn't wish that time on anyone. I'm not a criminal and never have been, yet people in this country were able to make my life a living hell.

I'm not a bitter person, and I don't hold grudges. I'm angry about what happened but I'll move on. I won't name names or try to extract revenge, and I won't roll around in the mud like those responsible for what happened. I'll stand tall instead and draw on the support of the people who mean more to me than anyone else.

CHAPTER 18

THE PEOPLE WHO COUNT

Everyone knows my brothers, Tom and Mike. Mike married early and moved to Dublin but he has a holiday home alongside Tom, back the road from me in Templenoe. Margaret, my sister, married a farmer in Kenmare, Arthur O'Sullivan, so she's close enough to us. With losing our father so young we rallied around each other and became very close, and we still are. Christmas Eve is here in this house for everyone, Christmas night is in Tommy's house, New Year's Eve in Margaret's. The nephews and nieces all get on great with each other, which is fantastic.

Mike has more All-Ireland medals than me at all levels. He was a brilliant corner-back with ferocious pace, and people barely know him. They used to say that John Egan was the most underrated forward in the game, but it was said so often that he wasn't underrated at all. But it's different for corner-backs. I remember one time looking at the famous 'Golden Years' video and Mike popped up maybe once coming out with the ball from defence. He never got the attention he deserved, but that's life for lads wearing the number two and number four jerseys.

He went into Norwich Union and married a girl from Dublin, Fiona Smyth. His son Darragh plays for Cuala and won an All-Ireland U21 medal with Dublin a couple of years ago, but Mike himself was unbelievably loyal to Templenoe. He's lived in Dalkey for years, but every Sunday he'd drive from Dublin to play for the club in Cahersiveen or Dromid or somewhere and then drive home afterwards.

And the thanks he got? He was dropped for a local final, a man with seven All-Ireland medals who drove the length of the country to play for the club. But that's how GAA clubs work.

I remember he was introduced one time to a prominent Kerry footballer who had no idea who he was. I said, 'Mike, why didn't you tell him you had four more All-Ireland medals than him?' That just wouldn't be his way at all.

Tommy is the businessman of the family, he's very successful in auctioneering and he bought the bar off me, so it's going to reopen after being closed for a few years. I had been approached to sell it and was offered a big price, but literally the same week Tommy approached me about buying it. I had been given the family silver by my mother, if you like, and it was only right to keep it in the family under the Spillane name. Now that it's reopened with the Spillane name over the door we're all delighted, and it'll give a great boost to the whole community. With Tommy's young lads getting involved, there should be another generation again running it, which is great.

Tommy was probably the best footballer of the three of us: pace, size, a rangy athlete, but he probably didn't have the interest we did. I was a lunatic in my focus but he was more focused on his business and he's done very well as a result.

Margaret is the rock of the family. I was chatting to someone one time about the ups and downs of my life and he pointed out that women have played a huge role in my life. He was right. My mother, Rosarii, my daughters, they all played or play a huge role in my life, and the same for Margaret. She made all the sacrifices while we were sent away to boarding school and left off to play football. She stayed at home, went to school in Kenmare and worked in the bar morning, noon and night. She drove that – and she's my mother to the core. My mother will never be dead as long as Margaret is alive. She has the look, the same as my mother and the same as my daughter Shona, which shows that it carries on through the generations.

Margaret went into nursing and ended as matron of Kenmare Hospital and married Arthur. Of course, as is typical with the GAA, when Kenmare played Templenoe, the O'Sullivans and the Spillanes used to have war but the enemies married in the end.

* * *

When Rosarii and I married we took over the bar and moved in. Tommy bought the house I live in now and my mother moved in there with him – but she kept an eye on us in the bar as well.

She would have expected us to work the same hours she had, no days off. If we took a night off she'd be back down to us the following day asking where we'd been. The same if we took an hour some evening to sit down for a cup of tea or to watch the TV.

One of our very first holidays as a married couple was a trip down to see Rosarii's parents in Enniscorthy. My mother rang to tell me to come home because there was a funeral and Rosarii cried all the way home in the car.

We had great times in the bar, absolutely, but it's a hard business and you're married to it. Rosarii had been in the hotel business, so she had a handle on the industry, but she often pointed out one telling difference. In a hotel there was job satisfaction – if someone had a nice stay, or a nice meal in the evening, they said thanks as they left.

In the bar, no one ever left saying, 'That was a great night, thanks for the lovely drinks.' That was a small thing she found hard enough.

Early on, if she was cross, she had a killer line to throw at me: 'I've only replaced your mother.' She was probably right. I'm useless. I was spoiled by my mother and I've been spoiled by Rosarii. She cooks and washes, but she also changes the plugs, does the painting – anything like that, she's the one who does it, not me.

She often said that if a man hit her or had an affair she would leave him, no second chances, but as our daughter Shona said to her once, 'Mam, if Dad had an affair, you'd have to organise it for him.' And she's right. I love her more now than when I met her first. That time I was still a footballer, so my appreciation has deepened since. I'm not a romantic – I'm red-raw useless with that stuff. I'd forget her birthday and our anniversary. At one stage, I bought her the same birthday present three years in a row, so she just took over and bought her own.

But while we're very comfortable in each other's company, we don't live in each other's pockets either. She's a very quiet person. We get plenty of invitations to this event and that event, but the *Living with Lucy* programme was an exception. The reasons I did the show? One, to show what I was really like as a person. Two, that we live in a modest bungalow with two ordinary cars, not in the lap of luxury.

And the main reason? To show off the beauty of Templenoe and the surrounding area.

What happened in reality was that years of me being stretched on the couch watching sport on the television came home to roost. In all those years, Rosarii would have been saying to me, 'We need a new carpet,' 'That door needs to be replaced,' and so on, but when we learned that a TV show was going to be broadcast from the house, we had to get years of jobs done in three weeks.

Another motivation for doing the show was the negativity and stress we'd been under for a couple of years; it was a bit of fun after having a tough time. I wanted to show off the area a bit, and I also wanted to show Rosarii off – our little bit of heaven.

She's private. Religious. She likes to walk but not with me, because she's too fast for me now.

After we got married in 1987, I never won another All-Ireland medal, so maybe there's a message there, but she's my soulmate. Absolutely. My rock. We've never fallen out or gone to bed at night arguing. Everything I've ever done, she's supported me. She's been with me for the highs and lows, she knows my moods inside out.

She gave up her career to rear the kids and she did all the driving to matches, all the parent-teacher meetings, the parties they went to, all of that. That was one thing Rosarii stressed – that we were going to devote our lives to rearing the children, to ensure they wanted for nothing and that we gave them every support we could, so that hopefully they would be able make careers and lives for themselves.

We reared the three of them the same, and they're completely different to each other. The first two were girls, which didn't please their granny too much, and it wasn't much fun for Rosarii to be hearing 'a boy or a child?' or 'when will ye go for the footballer?'

Granny had no time for girls. My first was Cara, and Margaret's first was Aoife, and they're the same age. That didn't go down well with Granny, particularly when they became independent girls who didn't care too much for Granny's opinion.

Cara is very independent, she always wanted to do her own thing. We'd go to the Dingle Skellig Hotel on holidays, and she was fascinated by a school across the harbour from the hotel – Coláiste Íde, an all-Irish boarding school, the only one of its kind in the country. She had no Irish but wanted to go to school there, so we left her over there. Boarding school is tough, as I knew well myself, but within three months she was fluent in Irish, fluent in Spanish, fluent in French. She was the only student in the school doing Spanish for her Leaving Cert and she did it through Irish, being taught by a Spanish girl who was a *gaeilgeoir*. Some set-up.

She went to UCC and qualified in law and Irish but had no interest in pursuing that – she went working for Emirates for three years, travelled to 65 countries and then came back to Dublin, landing in to work in PR and marketing. She works for one of the banks, and Gaelic games are part of her job. She probably knows more about what's going on in that regard than I do. Not hard, some might say. She lights up a room when she walks in and she's flying it. We're so proud of her.

Shona is different and has been different from the start. She arrived at 30 weeks, weighing less than three pounds. She fought to survive in the Bon Secours and she's been a fighter all her life. Totally different to Cara – Shona is quiet, introverted. Fell in love with a lovely chap in college, Liam Conway, and they got married a couple of years ago. She works as a nurse and was truly born to that job. She is an oncology clinical nurse specialist, which I would feel is a very challenging job, but she loves it and it suits her. She's often said to me that it's a beautiful privilege to work with a person at the end of their life.

She and Liam were supposed to get married on 20 June 2020. It was going to be a massive day but it had to be cancelled due to Covid. The day we were supposed to have the wedding, we had a ceremony of our own here. My son Pat dressed as a priest and our families were present to celebrate the day.

They finally got married in October 2020, when there were 50 allowed at a ceremony – we had 48 people. Rosarii's sisters couldn't even come. Ireland went into lockdown the following day, so she dodged a bullet. I mentioned the wedding in passing the following year in an interview with Marty Morrissey, that we had a beautiful day, and of course someone felt it necessary to text in that it was typical that Pat Spillane's daughter was able to break the lockdown. We didn't, of course, though you'd wonder what a person like that has going on in their lives that they'd find the time to text a radio programme about it.

Shona and Liam live in Cork and we visit them regularly – even more regularly now because a year and a half ago they gave us our first grandchild, Croía Conway. Last year, in the middle of the hullabaloo about ending *The Sunday Game* and so on, it was great just to have Croía rolling around the floor. She melts our hearts, and we're making good use of the new Macroom bypass to make the trip up.

Pat is our only boy, and when he was born, my mother was delighted: huge celebrations. I was at the birth, and the doctor said, 'Look at his hands, he'll be a footballer.' All the Spillanes would have big hands and that was the first thing the doctor noticed.

He has never given us a day's trouble. Very good at school, loved sport, and he's not his father's son. He's his own man. He was very good at soccer, and basketball was probably his best sport.

He's six foot three and blessed with a great engine – he'd be in the top 10 per cent of inter-county players in terms of fitness. I always believed he'd make it as a footballer because he had the raw materials. But he's had it tough in football.

First, he was called Pat Spillane, which meant tough comparisons. Second, the sins of his father would be visited on him. Third, it might have been better to be born in a city – the downside of rural Ireland is that it's parochial, and jealousy and begrudgery live here too.

Pat has suffered from all three as a result. He didn't make the Kerry underage teams and he wasn't a regular on the Templenoe senior team. He got a raw deal in both cases – with Kerry and the club I gave my life to. My initial impulse would be to give out and start naming names, to list the wrongs committed against him, but I won't. I don't want to settle grudges.

Managing teams is hard. Selectors and managers are entitled to their opinions and to make their own decisions. But I went to Kerry minor trials and he should have been on the Kerry minor panel. I saw Templenoe games and felt he should have been on the senior team in the club. As an objective judge of football, I felt he should have been on those teams. But I'm his father, and people would only expect me to say that.

I was thrilled he got into sport and into Gaelic football in particular. Sport has so many advantages, so many benefits, that it's wonderful but also cruel. And at a small parochial level it can be its cruellest. As a teacher, I always tried to take the holistic approach, the person all in all. But in sport, and the GAA is no better than any other sport, the holistic approach counts for nothing. It's all about winning

THE PEOPLE WHO COUNT

and too often it's about winning at all costs, not about developing a young person as a person, being positive, being constructive.

I saw that with the Kerry minors, when Pat got a text message to say, 'Sorry, you haven't made it.' I thought there was a better way than just a text. With the club there was little or no encouragement, no explanation of decisions. For those reasons Pat's football career from underage up until he was 23 was terrible. Rejection after rejection. Humiliation after humiliation. A young lad not getting a chance.

How he came through all of that, the substitutions, being dropped, a mistake and off the field immediately – I don't know how he kept going. We'd look out the window and see a fine strapping young lad coming in after a game with the head down and the shoulders drooped – you didn't have to ask how it had gone. He'd been taken off or not even gotten a game. It would have broken anyone.

He did trials for Australian Rules, and for a couple of years he held the record for the standing high jump and standing long jump because he was blessed with those explosive fast-twitch muscles. One of the AFL agents was always on to me because they could see the data from those tests and knew the raw material was there, but it always came back to the same questions: why didn't he play minor for Kerry and why can't he get on his club side?

I'd love to have answered that it wasn't quite that straightforward, but I couldn't. It's a pity he didn't get to Australia because I'm certain he would have made it, that that game would have suited him.

With UCC there was more rejection. He ended up pulling out of the Sigerson panel the same year UCC won it.

Then he moved away to Dublin. He was coming down to play games but he was only getting seven minutes here, nine minutes there, a league game maybe, but no sign of a start in the championship. He'd never be critical of Templenoe, but I was angry about that. I'd be biting my lip.

He came on in the All-Ireland intermediate club semi-final against Oughterard and he was outstanding, but that was bittersweet because he was leaving the club. He was finding it difficult to travel down for five minutes of a game, and he told his mother he was going to change club but he wasn't looking forward to telling me that news in case I was hurt.

He had made the decision to transfer to St Jude's in Dublin. And that was liberating for him, the feeling that he was going to make a fresh start with St Jude's. When he'd come on for Templenoe in the All-Ireland junior club final in 2016, he'd scored a point and I got a great kick out of that. By the same token, I remember him at one training session for the All-Ireland intermediate club final in the field in Templenoe, and I cried watching him from the car outside the field. I couldn't understand why a man of his stature, with huge speed and a great kick, had to leave his club because he couldn't get his game. He didn't deserve that.

He went from being a sub with Templenoe at intermediate to playing in Croke Park and being selected as one of the GAA players of the week just two years later. They talk about Dublin clubs poaching players, particularly lads from the country who end up in Dublin, but he wound up with St Jude's because a friend of Cara's was going with a St Jude's player. It was also the closest club to where he lived.

When he joined, Gareth Roche, the manager of St Jude's, rang him and said he'd love to meet him for a coffee. They met for two hours because Gareth wanted to find out about him, his ambitions, his background, all of that.

He started with the intermediates in Jude's, then worked his way into the senior team, and then he played in the Dublin county semi-final and final in 2021: he was man of the match in the semi. From being a sub on an intermediate team, he ended up man of the match in a senior semi-final and playing centre-field in Croke Park for Sligo as well as being nominated as one of the GAA's three players of the week.

I couldn't say enough good things about St Jude's. They gave him coaching for the first time, but they also gave him confidence, belief and a chance. That's what every youngster wants.

Before lining out for Jude's the manager said to him, 'We don't care what happened in Templenoe, we don't want to know what happened there. What you need to know is, next Saturday night, if you kick a ball wide, you're not going to be taken off.' It was a vote of confidence.

As a result of that, Sligo got in touch because Rosarii is from Sligo. Her family weren't involved directly in the GAA but they were involved in Scór through the Carrowroe club. Rosarii and her sisters have a Connacht medal for ballad singing, while Helena, another sister, has an All-Ireland medal for solo singing.

Pat is living the dream. He's happy he got his chance. I used to tell the Aussie Rules agent that he was a raw, uncut diamond, that he just needed polishing. Or confidence, maybe.

Sligo were great to give him that confidence, that belief. The message from the management has always been simple and direct: just do your thing. I'm delighted to see that the belief we always had in him is now shared by others.

It was no different with me. My strengths were my kicking and my engine; Pat has a much better top speed and is a better kicker, but the difference is I got a chance with a successful team, and he's only now getting his chance with Sligo. But sitting in Croke Park last year with him starting centre-field for Sligo against Cavan in the Tailteann Cup – that was special. I'd have died happy after it.

He's a brand manager now with a drinks company, so he's successful in his career also. What he's achieved has not been because he's Pat Spillane's son. He's earned it all himself.

The three of them can all say the same, and we're very proud of them.

* * *

The day I stood on the rock in the O'Sheas' garden to see my father's funeral cortège leave the churchyard is a long, long time ago now. It saddens me that he missed so much of our childhoods, which was of course part of the reason I cried on *The Sunday Game* in 2022.

I take consolation in the fact that my mother lived to see so many of the great times, when the Spillane name became famous all over Ireland and when a small rural place a few miles outside Kenmare was associated with the greatest days in Irish sport. That's the key to everything: my family and my home place of Templenoe, which are practically the same for me.

I often wonder what my father would have made of how Templenoe has changed and how it's stayed the same. And how his children changed and how they've stayed the same. I like to think of him watching his children and his grandchildren as they make their way, both in the home place he loved and in places far away from it alike. The fact that all of them come back the road to Templenoe so regularly would surely gladden his heart.

ACKNOWLEDGEMENTS

M y thanks to all the people who've helped me over the years in all sorts of ways. If I were to start thanking every one of them now I'd fill another book.

My father, Tom, and mother, Maura, gave me and my brothers and sister a wonderful childhood in Templenoe. I owe everything to them, and my mother in particular for her selflessness over many years rearing us on her own.

My brothers, Tom and Mike, soldiered with me for Templenoe and Kerry, while my sister, Margaret, is the anchor of the family now in the same way my mother was. I have always been grateful to them all for their love and support.

I have given decades to Templenoe GAA club and was always proud to wear the blue and white jersey. I thank my clubmates for their staunch support in good times and bad.

The same to the men who wore the green and gold with me in fields all over Ireland. As I say in this book, nothing can take away the respect I have for my Kerry teammates.

The staff and pupils at Bantry VS/St Goban's were always supportive, a special group of people over the years – I enjoyed every day I spent teaching in the town.

My colleagues on *The Sunday Game* in RTÉ were as diverse a group as the pupils and teachers in Bantry, and just as good to work with. The producers, presenters, pundits and others made the experience an enjoyable one for decades.

Particular thanks to Sarah Liddy of Gill Books for her support and encouragement, and also to Michael Moynihan (and Marjorie, Clara, Bridget, Bobby and Breda) for his work.

I hope this book shows people who I really am as opposed to the impression they may have from seeing me on TV for a couple of hours a year. If so, they'll appreciate just how much family means to me – my children, Cara, Shona and Pat Junior; my son-in-law, Liam Conway; and my beautiful granddaughter, Croía, are everything to me, and I'm glad to get the chance to express that here.

Above all this book is dedicated to my wife, Rosarii. She has been there with me in good times and bad; she has been my rock ever since the first night I heard her in our old bar. That night she was singing the John Denver song 'Follow Me'. I've always been happy that I did.